VH1's 100 Greatest Albums

100 Greatest Albums

Edited by Jacob Hoye

BARNES & NOBLE BOOKS
NEW YORK

ACKNOWLEDGMENTS:
Gene Bolan, Barbara Chilenskas, Selene Costello, Linda Dingler, Dave Dunton, Walter Einenkel, Jim Fitzgerald, Andrea Glanz, Michael Grimes, Jade Hoye, Richard Hoye, Jessica Jones, J. P. Jones, Bernie Kaminsky, Lauren McKenna, Christina Norman, Donna O'Neill, Jim Petersen, Janet Rollé, Ann Sarnoff, Felisa Sgroi, Liate Stehlik, Alyssa Taragano, Nicole Tourtelot, WBOB, Nadja Webb, Eric Wybenga, and Nancy Abbott-Young.

Special thanks to Wenonah who always lets me choose the music in the car.

100 Greatest Albums

VH1's 100 Greatest Albums

Introduction

My earliest memory of hearing music, the mesmerizing kind that takes hold of you and won't let go, is sitting at the top of the stairs in the tiny townhouse I grew up in to listen to "Golden Slumbers." This is when I was four or five. The song had climbed out of the Scott hi-fi and up the stairs to compel me out of bed. Downstairs was the din of activity, my parents partying with friends or with each other, I don't recall. The music soon subsumed other sounds. It may have been midnight. It may only have been eight o'clock, but it felt like twilight. The song's rich piano, Paul McCartney's voice laying down the sweetest assurances, the majestic brass section rising like waves, made me feel ethereal as the band laid into the triumphantly existential "Boy! You're gonna carry that weight, carry that weight a long time!" I have. The epic suite unfurled into "The End," sending me off to bed with its great summation of the hippie dream.

That was the first of many times that *Abbey Road* would draw me to the top of the stairs to drift in the album's fantastical landscapes. To me, the album seemed to play itself out as some mysterious story about a kid named Little Darlin' traveling through a psychedelic world, like *Alice in Wonderland*. This was a child's musical.

"Maxwell's Silver Hammer" could be a Maurice Sendak tale. What kid wouldn't follow Ringo down to an octopus's garden in the shade? And with characters like Mean Mr. Mustard and Polythene Pam, the Beatles's world felt as darkly appealing as Dr. Seuss's. The album's final message, "And in the end, the love you take is equal to the love you make"—a comment on the human condition even a child can comprehend—has the same gorgeous simplicity as Shel Silverstein's *The Giving Tree.*

Years later, the hi-fi moved to my room and so did the album. *Abbey Road* and I started down a new path as I unlocked songs like "Come Together" and "I Want You (She's So Heavy)." To this day, *Abbey Road* is a presence in my life, an energy. Great albums have that characteristic. You can love a song, but you can form a bond with an album, a relationship that evolves as organically and beautifully as a marriage. Like people, there aren't all that many great ones, and few stand the test of time. But they're out there. This book has a hundred of them; albums that tackle the human experience, albums full of theatre, love, heartbreak, joy, grief, pride, spirituality, sadness, politics, poetics, and just about everything else that could fit on the bands of an LP and, now, a CD. They excite, educate, illuminate, and entertain. Like novels, plays, and paintings, they help us understand ourselves, and, sometimes, escape ourselves.

As you go through this list, you'll naturally find things with which to agree and disagree. It's part of the fun of constructing a list like this; perhaps it will encourage you to construct your own. Hopefully, we'll turn you on to albums you may have missed the first time around, or get you to apply fresh ears to old favorites.

The goal with these essays was not to produce capsule reviews or recapitulate what's been said a thousand times. After all, these albums have all been much discussed. Rather, we tried to apply a personal perspective to many of them to get at the emotional connection one makes with an album and to demonstrate the impact albums can have on a life.

Putting the list together was an overwhelming proposition, so VH1 sent ballots out to over 700 musicians, from Art Garfunkel to Britney Spears; songwriters, disc jockeys, radio programmers, and critics to vote on the one hundred greatest albums of rock and roll. The votes were calculated and the albums were ranked, producing the following list.

Enjoy.

Jacob Hoye

NYC 2003

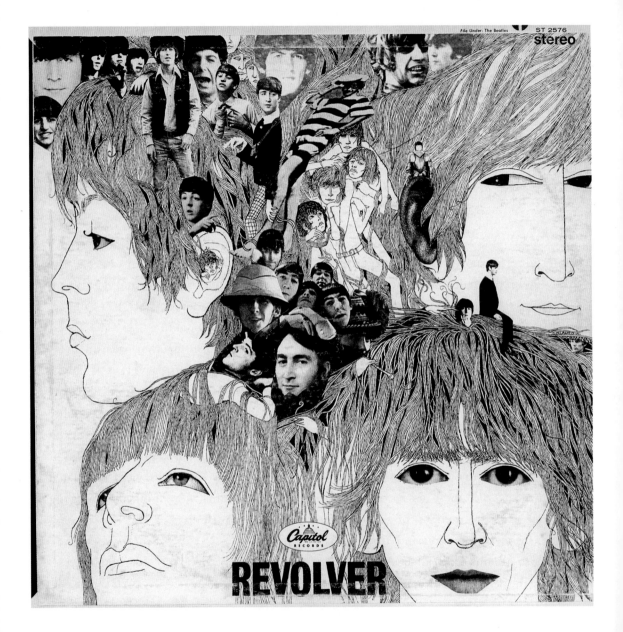

Revolver

Number one in any poll is a nearly impossible burden for any piece of music to bear. In the case of best album, there are plenty of contenders and counterarguments but *Revolver* is truly as good a choice as any. It's yet more proof, as if any were needed, that the Beatles remain an iconic and active force in popular music decades after their end.

Revolver at number one seems fitting, as it was actually the first album I ever bought with my own money. My best friend John Ross had a copy that had belonged to his father, and we'd sit around and flip baseball cards and talk about girls and what was cool for hours while it played on his old Realistic turntable. I realized eventually that I was going over to his house as much to hear the album as for any other reason, so I decided to get my own copy.

Several hundred album purchases down the line, *Revolver* has proven a very tough act to follow. It ranks without doubt among the finest of the Beatles's work, and despite their relatively short life the Beatles remain the

CAPITOL
1966

George Harrison:
vocals, guitar, sitar, tambourine, sound effects

John Lennon:
vocals, guitar, horn, marimbas, organ, tambourine, sound effects

Paul McCartney:
vocals, bass guitar, tambourine

Ringo Starr:
drums, vocals, tambourine

Various additional musicians

Produced by
George Martin

best band ever. Others have and will continue to do new things with rock and roll, but the Beatles will forever mark the form's high renaissance. These are the guys who figured it out, took it to another level, and defined it for generations to come.

Listen—as merely a collection of songs, *Revolver* is hard to beat: "Eleonor Rigby"; "Here, There, and Everywhere"; "Yellow Submarine"... like most Beatles albums, it could pass for a greatest hits collection. But *Revolver*'s historical context also needs to be taken into account.

It's 1966 and you're listening to *Revolver* for the first time. You've heard distortion on "(I Can't Get No) Satisfaction," feedback on "I Feel Fine," and vocal acrobatics from the Beach Boys. Lyrically, you've heard Dylan take things from "Chimes of Freedom" to "Desolation Row." But you've

The Beatles will forever mark the form's high renaissance. These are the guys who figured it out and took it to another level and defined it for generations to come.

got the new Beatles album on your turntable and you probably didn't expect it to start out with a disembodied voice mumbling "One, two, three, four . . ." accompanied by tape-sped guitar sounds and a cough.

You may have been surprised, too, to hear the Beatles give way to the chamber music accompaniment of "Eleanor Rigby," and you might really begin to wonder once you hit the backward solo on "I'm Only Sleeping." Somewhere in the middle of George Harrison rocking out on sitar in "Love You To," it probably occurs to you that rock and roll has taken a strange new road. (And *Revolver* is, in many ways, George's album. For the first time, he contributes three songs, and his exposure to eastern tonalities and instrumentation permeate the piece as a whole. What's more, he shreds throughout.)

Of course, you may well have been on this road already. If you, like the Beatles, had been turned on by 1966—as it was called in that more iridescent time—you may have grokked on the fact that the fab four evidently had been as well.

The Beatles's achievement, with *Revolver,* was in expressing the psychedelic experience aurally. From that album on, sitars and backward-masking have stood as musical shorthand for '60s psychedelia, and psychedelic '60s music is what *Revolver* played a mighty role in spawning. That, and a lot .more; thirty-six years later, the Chemical Brothers are opening their shows with a loop from "Tomorrow Never Knows" that feels right at home in its new setting.

More than anything, the Beatles with *Revolver* declared rock and roll to be a wide-open field, something that could encompass the orchestral and the eastern, the romantic, the transcendental, and the whimsical. They accomplished this through the songs but also through some of the most innovative and gorgeous production heard then or since (for which George Mar-

tin must also be mentioned). It is an album that sounds quite unlike anything else, even prior or subsequent work by the Beatles. *Revolver* exists in its own universe, on a knife's edge between rock and roll and rock.

But I wasn't thinking about these thing when I listened to *Revolver* all those years ago. What I was thinking was: What amazing songs, and the whole album's good. Each of those two- to three-minute songs contained worlds. Listening to the CD now, I'm struck once again at how accomplished they were, how groundbreaking their sound and style was, how fine their songwriting. And despite all the weight of hype and history, they're really not overrated.

Music changed the day that *Revolver* was released, forever and for better. There's not many albums you can say that about. If you're lucky enough to come upon it early in your own listening life, it will change you, too. Unfortunately, it also sets an impossibly high standard for whatever follows. You'll leap with eagerness into the thicket, but you won't find many more this good. E.W.

Nevermind

You don't skip through songs when you listen to *Nevermind*. You listen to it one after another. It's almost like you're cheating yourself if you don't listen to one song.

—BILLIE JOE ARMSTRONG, GREEN DAY

The thought that a flannel T-shirt and an unshaven face could be viewed as revolutionary and/or iconoclastic just didn't cross our minds.

I'm from Seattle. I should get that out of the way right off the bat. Due to our proximity to it all, we Seattleites have an entirely different perspective on this whole thing that Nirvana started. We simply weren't as in awe of them as the rest of the world was. The thought that a flannel T-shirt and an unshaven face could be viewed as revolutionary and/or iconoclastic just didn't cross our minds. We laughed when designer Marc Jacobs and the *New York Times* repurposed Kurt Cobain's vehement antifashion statement for the next big style thing.

Don't get me wrong; we loved the music. In fact, when the rest of the world caught on, we sort of felt as if our baby had been kidnapped. And though this album's importance in the grand scheme of things has been overblown in the light of Cobain's death, one thing's for sure: *Nevermind* sure did throw the whole entertainment biz for a loop. No one could've predicted that three unassuming, relatively camera-shy Seattle guys would leave an indelible mark on the radio airwaves, the music channels, the fashion and antiperspirant worlds.

Nevermind was most of the world's introduction to the band, but it was, in fact, their second album. *Bleach*, which came out on Sub Pop in 1989, introduced the world to a pissed-off, intelligent sound that was more dynamic than metal, less balls-out irreverence than punk, and more poetic than both. It's a sound they honed and perfected—with the help of producer Butch Vig—on *Nevermind.*

In a fitting tribute to the sudden explosion that they sparked with their "arrival," *Nevermind* opens with the pow-bang hit single "Smells Like Teen Spirit." Not much can be said about this album that hasn't already been said, but it bears repeating that even Nirvana didn't realize what a powder keg they had in this song. Kurt thought he was just riffing on a piece of graffiti written by queen riot grrl/Bikini Kill singer Kathleen Hanna, but it turns out he was

GEFFEN RECORDS
1991

Kurt Cobain:
vocals, guitars
Kris Novelselic:
bass
Dave Grohl:
drums

Produced by
Butch Vig

speaking to an entire generation of bored adolescents.

The rest is history. They say imitation is the sincerest form of flattery, and the bombastic, rough-around-the edges sound—a sound that would soon come to be known as "grunge"—is often imitated, but yet to be duplicated. Ironically, this singular sound was itself borne of flattery. Kurt confesses to having modeled "Teen Spirit" on a Pixies song. While the Pixies rarely even make a showing on these sorts of best-of lists, without them, there could be no Nirvana.

When Kurt committed suicide in 1994, three short years after their debut, many of us couldn't help but notice the eerily prophetic messages in his lyrics. One track that sends shivers down the spine is "Come As You Are," in which Kurt seems to be raising his right hand while crossing his fingers behind his back as he "swears" that he doesn't have a gun. To this day the urban legends inspired by Nirvana lyrics are rivaled only by the pot-fueled conspiracy theories that surround those of Led Zeppelin or the Beatles.

That's about as legendary as it gets.   C.R.

The Beach Boys Pet Sounds

Sloop John B./ Caroline No
Wouldn't It Be Nice/You Still Believe In Me
That's Not Me/Don't Talk (Put Your Head on My Shoulder)
I'm Waiting For The Day/Let's Go Away For Awhile
God Only Knows/I Know There's An Answer/Here Today
I Just Wasn't Made For These Times/Pet Sounds

Capitol
RECORDS

Pet Sounds

Pet Sounds is an unbelievable record. It's like classical music. Wonderful compositions, beautiful singing. I think the compositions stand up to any kind of interpretation. I've heard "Put Your Head On My Shoulder" played on the cello and it sounds like a piece of music that's been with us for hundreds and hundreds of years. It sounds like it's always been there. And I think maybe in a hundred years' time people will be playing their songs on the piano trying to work out where they came from.

—ELVIS COSTELLO

CAPITOL
1966
Brian Wilson:
vocals, piano, bass
Mike Love:
keyboards, vocals
Carl Wilson:
guitar, vocals
Al Jardine:
guitar, vocals
Dennis Wilson:
drums, vocals
Produced by
Brian Wilson

As rock's preeminent headcase, Brian Wilson has always been an enigmatic figure. In musical terms, at least 90 percent of his mystique rests on this record—for few albums have inspired as many imitators as *Pet Sounds*. Coming as it did in the spring of 1966, it can be seen as perhaps the first self-conscious attempt at crafting an LP as an LP. Considering that most albums at that time, save for perhaps the ones made by the Beatles and Bob Dylan, consisted of hit singles surrounded by obvious filler, *Pet*

Sounds was a giant step toward artistic freedom in the name of rock 'n' roll. The key phrase here is "self-conscious." Wilson had already established himself as a songwriter and producer of towering repute, but the strictures inherent in the Beach Boys facade had become problematic to him, simply because the sounds he was hearing in his head—in many cases brought about by the large amount of marijuana and LSD he was ingesting—had become too complex for the rigid structure of the group.

> *The sounds he was hearing in his head—in many cases brought about by the large amount of marijuana and LSD he was ingesting—had become too complex for the rigid structure of the group.*

Because of this dilemma, Wilson brought in a whole new fleet of behind-the-scenes whizzes for *Pet Sounds*. The Boys remained the Boys in name only. Using studio musicians was not uncommon in the sixties, particularly in L.A.—but *Pet Sounds* was different because it was planned from the beginning as a thematic whole and the musicians were merely snap-in components. While the original Beach Boys all sang on *Pet Sounds*, the music was, for the most part, played by session men. This gave Brian a more autocratic role in the album's execution. Brian had also brought in a composing partner named Tony Asher to share the songwriting duties, which made *Pet Sounds* even less of a Beach Boys album than ever. The songs themselves were deeply personal, sometimes expressing troubling visions and reflective insecurities that were new turf for a group whose fun-and-sun anthems had, until now, been mostly on the light side (despite the fact that, even as far back as "In My Room" in 1963, Brian had shown signs of a more troubled disposition lurking underneath). The public reacted negatively—*Pet Sounds* was the least successful Beach Boys album to date, barely scraping the Top 10. This indifference was perhaps the single factor that drove Wilson to new heights of paranoia and anxiety. As a result, he was never again able to match the pinnacle of *Pet Sounds*.

More than anything else, *Pet Sounds* was about loss of innocence. The opening track, "Wouldn't It Be Nice," presented a scenario of suburban fulfillment, but as idyllic as it sounded, the lyrics betrayed Wilson's underlying sense of insecurity. "That's Not Me" came right out with an almost psychiatrist's-couch type of soul searching that matched its title, all to the accompaniment of the ultimate sixties L.A. studio concoction: immense echo chambers, sleighbells, assorted percussion, light trumpets, tympani, and other effects—effects that would no doubt influence efforts like the Beatles' *Sgt. Pepper's Lonely Hearts Club Band.* Even "Sloop John B," which, on the surface, sounded like a jaunty sea chantey, lamented: "This is the worst trip I've ever been on." The swirling psychedelic effects led one to believe the "trip" in question might not be strictly a nautical voyage. And in "I Just Wasn't Made for These Times," Wilson's escapist tendencies are more pronounced than ever, only this time he doesn't want to merely retreat to his room—or the sandbox—but would rather escape the sixties altogether.

By far, *Pet Sounds'* crowning achievement was the majestic "Caroline, No," which summed up the coming-of-age insecurity that seemed to lie at the core of the album. The message was that life from here on out—that is, postadolescence—would be a series of bittersweet complexities. This fact was borne out by the brilliantly understated texture of the music, which glistened like the last dying minutes of a late summer day. Since the Beach Boys—or, more specifically, Brian Wilson—were never capable of recapturing the peak attained by this album, in many ways, this song, which was the last one on the LP, was the final sundown. It's not surprising that Wilson later dubbed it "God's music."

Thirty-five years later, the choir is still singing. J.S.H.

STEREO

what's
going on

MARVIN GAYE

TS310

ORCHESTRA CONDUCTED
AND ARRANGED BY
DAVID VAN DePITTE

What's Going On

4

What's Going On signifies an album of a guy that artistically had to say what he had to say, no matter what anybody else said, and, to me, it signifies what an album and an artist should be about.   —CHUCK D

Many critics, artists, and music fans have called Marvin Gaye's *What's Going On* the greatest soul album ever made, and some have gone even further, claiming it is the greatest album ever made, period. Whether one agrees with either judgment, this 1971 classic remains, undeniably, one of the most moving and masterful suites of music ever conceived. Gaye achieved many pinnacles during his hit-studded and genre-defining career, but *What's Going On* is undoubtedly the highest. The LP possesses a graceful artistry, an unswerving sense of purpose, and a deep-seated spirituality that seized the zeitgeist of its time, but will never go out of style.

It is said that momentous victories can only come with enormous cost and effort, and that is certainly true of this

MOTOWN RECORDS
1971
Marvin Gaye:
vocals, drums,
keyboards, piano
**Earl Van Dyke,
Joe Messina,
Robert White:**
guitar
**Bob Babbitt, James
Jamerson:**
bass
**Eli Fountain,
Wild Bill Moore:**
sax
Produced by
Marvin Gaye

one. Ironically, a record of this magnitude could not have been undertaken at a more tumultuous or uncertain time in the artist's personal life and public career. At home, Gaye was in the midst of coping with the death of his longtime duet partner Tammi Terrell, his crumbling marriage to Anna Gordy, sister of Motown Records' president Berry Gordy, growing drug problems, and a slew of IRS-related affairs that were close to bankrupting him. Professionally, the Prince of Motown had reached the end of his rope when it came to playing up the suave lover man image his label openly cultivated. The frustrated singer wanted to create music that flew in the face of expectation and attempted to reconcile all the hurt and suffering he felt in the world around him. As far as he was concerned, he didn't want to sing another "I Heard It Through the Grapevine" or "How Sweet It Is (To Be Loved By You)" ever again, so when Obie Benson of the Four Tops and songwriter Al Cleveland brought Marvin a song that reflected the death of the sixties and the subsequent fallout, he leaped at the chance to prove himself a different kind of artist.

Gaye was in the midst of coping with the death of his longtime duet partner, his crumbling marriage, growing drug problems, and a slew of IRS-related affairs that were close to bankrupting him.

The song, after a few tweaks from Marvin, was "What's Going On" and it almost never came out. Gordy opposed Marvin's production and writing of his own material and furthermore didn't understand the overall concept of the album Gaye wanted to make. He flatly refused to release it, thinking it amounted to career suicide for Gaye, but the rebellious singer stood his ground and announced he wouldn't record anything else for the label until they gave "What's Going On" a chance. When the song topped the soul charts and hit number two on the pop charts, it gave Marvin the breathing room he needed to record the full album, which then saw release on May 21, 1971.

The set opens to the raw chatter of the studio musicians and, then, the swooning saxophone lick that would forever be remembered. The soul-searching title cut signifies everything about the artist's new change in direction—lyrically, artistically, and vocally. Marvin pioneered a new multilayered singing style that would be the hallmark of the latter half of his career, when engineer Ken Sands accidentally played back two different vocal takes simultaneously. Lyrically, *What's Going On* is steeped with deeply emotional and religious overtones as Marvin writes what is essentially an open letter to God. He tackles environmental concerns on "Mercy Mercy Me (The Ecology)": "What about this overcrowded land / How much more abuse from man can she stand," drug abuse on "Flyin' High (In the Friendly Sky)": "Well I know I'm hooked my friend / To

the boy who makes slaves out of men," the future of humankind with "Save the Children": "Who's willing to try to save a world / That's destined to die," and the social uprisings of the time with "Inner City Blues (Make Me Wanna Holler)": "Make me wanna holler / The way they do my life." Though he would later return to the sensual themes that made him Motown royalty, Marvin would produce and write most of his work from that point onward. Sadly, as he gained more artistic control, his grip on his personal life disintegrated, ultimately leading to his untimely death in 1984 at the hand of his own enraged father the day before his forty-fifth birthday.

Three generations later, *What's Going On* still retains the same incredible power that made it so widely loved and praised at the time of its original release. It is a truly overwhelming and transcendent album, never failing to astonish those seeking hope, insight, solace, or simply some of the most soulful soul there ever was.

N.M.

Are You Experienced?

5

I don't think there is anything that even compares to that album. If you're not understanding that album—you don't really understand the main thrust of rock and roll.

—LIZ PHAIR

> **REPRISE**
> 1967
> **Jimi Hendrix:**
> vocals, guitars
> **Noel Redding:**
> bass, vocals
> **Mitch Mitchell:**
> drums, vocals
> **Produced by**
> Chas Chandler

The greatest debut album of the rock era. A psychedelic masterpiece. The most significant and influential demonstration in the history of the electric guitar's talismanic power. An essential document of sixties pop culture. *Are You Experienced?* is all these things, and many more. But its most astonishing quality, the one that keeps us returning to it more than thirty-five years after its release, is its giddy sense of unlimited freedom.

Right from the first, gloriously discordant guitar notes that kickstart "Purple Haze," the genius of Jimi Hendrix hurls itself at us, fully formed. He is the epitome of confidence, capable of whatever he sets his mind to, and his mind is telling him to make sounds unlike any previously made—or heard—by human beings. The band latches onto a dirty, devastating groove, then stops short. Hendrix calls out those famous words, " 'Scuse me while I kiss the sky," and as his overdriven Fender Stratocaster comes wailing back in, it's easy to believe he's actually doing that.

Back in 1967, it seemed to most people that Hendrix's talent had emerged out of nowhere. In actuality, he'd served as an apprentice for years, playing guitar with the likes of Little Richard, the Isley Brothers, and Curtis Knight. And he'd been trying, without much success, to make a go of a solo career on the coffeehouse circuit in New York's Greenwich Village. But it was only when Chas Chandler, ex-bassist of British R&B group the Animals and aspiring manager, met Hendrix and brought him to London in 1966 that the real transformation occurred.

That transformation was rapid indeed.

Hendrix makes his guitar howl like a hurricane, roar like a division of armored personnel carriers, and ring like a celestial siren.

Fixed up with a sympathetic backing band consisting of guitarist-turned-bassist Noel Redding and the brilliant Mitch Mitchell on drums, Hendrix took London by storm in a matter of months. And no wonder: He was a virtuoso guitar player, a powerful singer, and a dazzling showman, often playing his Strat with his teeth or behind his back. He also looked like no one else; wild-haired black American men dressed in velvet suits and frilly shirts weren't exactly common in mid-sixties England, or anywhere else for that matter.

One thing Hendrix wasn't was a song-writer. But that changed quickly too. All the songs on *Are You Experienced?*, save his reworking of "Hey Joe," were written following his arrival in England. "Manic Depression," "Love or Confusion," "Fire," "The Wind Cries Mary," "Foxy Lady"—

one classic followed another in a creative outpouring that remains staggering to this day. Blending the gritty blues of Muddy Waters and the subtle soul of Curtis Mayfield with the surrealism of Bob Dylan and the aggression of British bands like Cream and the Who, Hendrix came up with a style all his own: witty, expansive, moving, vicious, and way, way out there.

You could put some of this down to the drugs; the lyrics of the album's title track, and particularly its closing line, "Not necessarily stoned, but . . . beautiful," left little doubt that Jimi's mind had been chemically expanded. But acid and pot on their own can't explain the blossoming of Hendrix as an artist. The simple fact was that he heard music in a different way from everyone else.

Luckily, by 1967, recording studio technology had advanced to the point where it could capture what he heard—just barely, when stretched to the limit. Luckier still, Hendrix had henchmen who understood what he was going for. Inspired by his drive to find new sounds, engineer Eddie Kramer and effects technician Roger Mayer revolutionized record production and established a new sonic benchmark for rock. In the three-plus decades since this music was made, we've gotten used to hearing weird noises on records. But even so, the swirling backward tracks on "Are You Experienced?," the dramatic crossfades at the end of "I Don't Live Today," and the eerie slowed-down voices that lurk on the edges of "Third Stone from the Sun" have lost none of their boldness.

Boldest of all is Hendrix's own performance. He makes his guitar howl like a hurricane, roar like a division of armored personnel carriers, and ring like a celestial siren. As Redding pumps murkily underneath him and Mitchell eggs him on with maniacal rolls and flourishes, Hendrix crosses over into a place that only the most inspired musicians ever reach, a region without boundaries, where anything is possible. The sound he creates is the sound of liberation. And even though the young man who created it was sadly not long for this world, it frees us still. M.R.

Rubber Soul

6

"I get it," Bob Dylan said when the Beatles played him *Rubber Soul,* "you don't want to be cute anymore."

From its distorted cover photo to its punny title, *Rubber Soul* signals the Beatles' eagerness to try something different. A transitional album in almost every way, it gives birth to the Beatles' studio-bound mature period (they'd tour only one more time after its release) and a new style of songwriting that, while no less inspired than the paint-by-numbers pop that preceded it, would reveal a deeper layer of emotion than what had come before. It's the first of their arty albums—and the first conceived as an album and not a vehicle for hit singles, rock 'n' roll cover versions, or songs written to order for their movies.

The Beatles in 1965 were bullet-proof, three years into their reign as the biggest phenomenon pop had ever seen. Yet they were growing out of their lovable mop-top image and wanted their music to reflect it. Their second

> **CAPITOL**
> 1965
>
> **John Lennon:**
> guitar, tambourine, vocals
>
> **Paul McCartney:**
> bass, guitar, piano, vocals
>
> **George Harrison:**
> guitar, sitar, tambourine, vocals
>
> **Ringo Starr:**
> drums, Hammond organ, tambourine, vocals
>
> **Mal Evans:**
> Hammond organ
>
> **George Martin:**
> harmonium, piano, tambourine
>
> **Produced by**
> George Martin

movie, *Help!*, was a financial success, but the group was less than satisfied artistically with both the film and its songs—which, considering such classics as the title track and "Ticket to Ride," is saying a mouthful.

The music on *Rubber Soul* was a response to Dylan and the Byrds, while at the same time showing an appreciation for Motown and Memphis soul and the ability to fuse exotic elements such as the sitar music that first popped up on the *Help!* soundtrack before making "Norwegian Wood" the most innovative pop song of its moment. On *Rubber Soul* the rockers have a soft edge and the ballads have a strong beat. Many of the songs are more complex rhythmically and more swaggeringly hard-edged than anything the group had attempted before—yet they all sound like Beatle songs.

The album was banged out quickly—it

Through the course of fourteen songs, the singer is arrogant, jaded, pissed-off, bored, sullen, self-absorbed. The love affairs are mostly dysfunctional.

wasn't a Big Statement labored on for months like *Revolver* or *Sgt. Pepper*—and its innovations are subtle and all kept within the strict confines of the verse-chorus-bridge pop song the Beatles had been working in since day one. Recording began on October 12, 1965, and the album was released on December 3, in time for Christmas. The fourteen songs of the original English album clock in at just over thirty-five minutes.

Yet this is an album that would change the idea of what a pop album should be, how deep it should go, how the listener should feel about the singer, stuff like that. It also boasts great song after great song in a bunch of complementary styles.

This is the first album where the Beatles don't seem like nice guys. Their image isn't pleasant. Through the course of fourteen songs, the singer is arrogant, jaded, pissed-off, bored, sullen, self-absorbed. The love affairs are mostly dysfunctional, from the McCartney breakup songs "I'm Looking Through You" and "You Won't See Me" to Lennon's more violent "Run for Your Life" and "Norwegian Wood." Even "Michelle," the adult contemporary pop tune (a big deal at the time—the Beatles writing standards) has a touch of melancholy, a language barrier that causes a literal failure to communicate.

The Beatles made a big step on *Rubber Soul* by recording nonlove songs, which may not seem like a big deal now, but was in the Top 40 arena they were working in. "Nowhere Man" is the first of what would become a string of what-a-fucked-up-guy-I-am lyrics Lennon would write for the rest of his life, aided by a gorgeous twelve-string guitar lead. In "Think for Yourself," Harrison, a bit self-righteously, urges the listener (and himself, maybe) to step off life's merry-go-round and meditate—"try thinking more if just for your own sake"; paradoxically, it's the album's hardest rocker. "In My Life" famously equates love with friendship, and "The Word" is about love of a more universal kind.

Rubber Soul is the most low-key of all the Beatles' great albums—and as such it's the one you'd be least likely to play at a party, but most likely to hole up with after something's gone wrong in your life. It's rock's first singer-songwriter album. And in a way, it's rock's first album, the first time a band created an album to be a complete listening experience. Sure, Sinatra had done that before, and Dylan with *Highway 61 Revisited.* But once the Beatles did it, no other rock band looked at its music the same way. The Beach Boys would record *Pet Sounds* in the next year, the Rolling Stones would cut *Aftermath,* the Kinks would make *Face to Face. Rubber Soul* made all that happen.

But why is it great? Try "Drive My Car," "Norwegian Wood," "You Won't See Me," "Nowhere Man"—and those are just the first four cuts. With its mix of randiness and introspection, its blend of folk, soul, and exotica, and its artfully focused energy, *Rubber Soul* represents the fullest flower of mid-sixties rock.   S.C.

Songs in the Key of Life

The first album that I could really remember in my household was Stevie Wonder's *Songs in the Key of Life*. It was about love. It was about life. It was about what was going on in the world.

—MARY J. BLIGE

Discovering this new direction and feeling a general discontent with Motown's strict regimen for his career, the prodigy turned prodigal rebelled when his contract was up and held the masters for his next two albums as leverage until the label gave him complete artistic control.

When Stevie Wonder set out to create what would become *Songs in the Key of Life,* he not only wanted to make the most ambitious album of his career, he wanted to pen a pioneering soul set that would rival the epic scope of labelmate Marvin Gaye's 1971 landmark opus *What's Going On.* Gaye had shattered the public's expectations and set new precedents for the genre, encouraging Wonder to explore the reaches of his own considerable talent.

Only eleven when he scored his first hit with "Fingertips (Pt. 2)" in 1962, Stevie Wonder was Motown's wunderkind, dutifully dispatching a series of sentimental and sunshiny hits for the majority of the sixties. However, as the era drew to a close, Wonder took on a more socially conscious tone when he recorded a touching rendition of Dylan's epochal "Blowin' in the Wind," a gesture that forever earned him a place in the heart of the Vietnam generation. Discovering this new direction and feeling a general discontent with Motown's strict

MOTOWN RECORDS
1976
Stevie Wonder:
keyboards, harmonica, vocals
Various musicians
Produced by
Stevie Wonder

regimen for his career, the prodigy turned prodigal rebelled when his contract was up and held the masters for his next two albums as leverage until the label gave him complete artistic control. The record company relented and the following five years would be the most creative and fruitful of the artist's career, yielding no less than six albums, culminating with Wonder's self-proclaimed *pièce de résistance*.

A sprawling twenty-one song collection, *Songs in the Key of Life* would become the definitive Stevie Wonder album, one that demonstrated a master at his peak. Accommodated over the course of two LPs and a bonus EP, the blind maestro swerved between pop and politics with a deft hand that demonstrated his immense skill as a songwriter and performer. "Love's in Need of Love Today" and "Village Ghetto Land" echoed Gaye's soul-searching sentiments of *What's Going On*, while "Black Man" tackled the inequities and ironies of racism in America. Somewhat ironically, it was the lighter fare, in the form of "Sir Duke," a tribute to the great Duke Ellington, and "I Wish," a reminiscing ode to innocent childhood days gone by, that helped Stevie score the biggest chart hits. In retrospect, however, *Songs in the Key of Life* will always be remembered as an album, not just the packaging for a few hit singles, and that's what Wonder wanted.

Sampled by everyone from Will Smith to Coolio, covered by such diverse vocalists as Aretha Franklin and Engelbert Humperdinck, and openly worshipped by new rising stars like Alicia Keys and Musiq, Wonder remains an institution of soul. One need go only as far as the radio dial to hear echoes of this master resonate through popular culture today, even as we turn back to his own great accomplishments for comfort and enlightenment. N.M.

Abbey Road

Rodgers and Hammerstein would've bowed to what was going on there in the shuffling of the tunes. It's very free and creative in how to break down traditional album making.

—ART GARFUNKEL

By this time it was almost over. The Beatles, who had changed the face of popular music from a weening pup to a multiheaded dragon breathing fire from every snout, were almost ready to call it quits after seven years of well-executed dominance. Their sheen shone like the sun. They were untouchable and remained that way to their last dying gasp . . . of which *Abbey Road* was the final grandiloquent utterance. Furthermore, it was actually *conceived* that way—although the botched fake-live *Let It Be* actually came out after *Abbey Road*, it was recorded months earlier. *Abbey Road* could have amounted to little more than an afterthought, given the malaise that had set upon the group by that time—a malaise wrought from not only years of being together and being the preeminent superstars in the rock arena but also a weariness brought about by intricate business dealings, deaths, and complex love affairs that had all ultimately taken their toll on the musical focus of the band. However, because the Beatles were consummate professionals, the album evolved into much more than that. It became an eloquent grand finale from the greatest group in the world.

Arguments prevail as to whether it was actually *too* slick—it's true, the Beatles had never known such a seamless level of gloss before. The very clean production was symptomatic of the kind of ultra-professionalism that would inevitably come to dominate in the seventies. But because they were the Beatles, it was still ultimately about *songs,* and like any Beatles album, *Abbey Road* was chock full of good ones. The suite-like grandeur of the second side—where each song sinuously flowed into the next—was an innovation in itself. Credit Paul McCartney for this—he was the one cobbling the group together, at least as far as maintaining the facade that the group was capable of any sort of unity at this point. *Abbey Road* was the last time any such unity existed.

Lennon's work on the album is angry and shows the new rad-lib direction that had been set upon him by his new muse-*cum*-wife, Yoko Ono. The avant-garde influence makes itself

APPLE
1969
John Lennon:
guitar, vocals
Paul McCartney:
bass, guitar,
piano, vocals
George Harrison:
guitar, vocals
Ringo Starr:
drums, vocals
Billy Preston:
organ
Mike Vickers:
Moog synthesizer
Produced by
George Martin

apparent in not only the cut-up lyrical pastiche of the manifesto-like "Come Together" but also the abrupt ending of "I Want You (She's So Heavy)," which is one of the first examples of the "primal scream" vocal style that Lennon would explore further on his first few solo albums.

Abbey Road also represented a genuine coming-of-age for the youngest Beatle, George Harrison, at least as far as songwriting went. Although Harrison had always remained in the shadows of Lennon/McCartney in this regard (given the immense productivity of said duo, who wouldn't?), on *Abbey Road* he proved himself capable of competing in the same stakes as far as writing perfectly hummable pop ditties went: "Here Comes the Sun" and "Something" became instant classics, covered by thousands of artists.

Any way you look at it, *Abbey Road* was the swansong-to-end-all-swansongs. Within a few months, the Beatles would be gone, but not forgotten. Albums like this are the reason why.

J.S.H.

Blonde on Blonde

9

COLUMBIA
1966
Bob Dylan:
guitar, harmonica,
keyboards, piano, vocals
Bill Atkins:
keyboards
Wayne Butler:
trombone
**Kenneth A. Buttrey
& Sanford Konikoff:**
drums
Rick Danko:
bass, violin, vocals
Paul Griffin:
piano
Garth Hudson:
keyboards, saxophone
Jerry Kennedy & Joe South:
guitar
Al Kooper:
guitar, horn,
keyboards, organ
Richard Manuel:
drums, keyboards, vocals
Charlie McCoy:
bass, guitar, trumpet
Wayne Moss:
guitar, vocals
Hargus "Pig" Robbins:
keyboards, piano
Robbie Robertson:
guitar, vocals
Henry Strzelecki:
bass
Produced by
Bob Johnston

I must have five copies of that record now. And every time you play it it sounds exceptional. It's unusually constructed, as if all the unessential things have been stripped away. Yet it's quite chaotic as well at times. Sounds improvised, but I don't think it was improvised. I think that was just a very particular frame of mind and that sells it.

—ELVIS COSTELLO

Although no one knew it at the time, this was to be the last of Dylan's great mid-sixties mind-bombs. It was his third breakthrough album in little more than a year, and in his spare time Dylan had taken to the road with the Band and annihilated whatever trappings remained of his urban-waif folksinging image of a few years before—along the way stirring controversy and exploding expectations of how a pop star should look, sound, and behave. The new-model Dylan was druggy and sardonic, his songs kaleido-scopes of hallucinatory imagery and disillusioned bile laid atop a uniquely astringent blues-rock terrain that no one had attempted, and which no one has touched since.

Blonde on Blonde was recorded when Dylan was engaged in the project of living out the apex of the Dylan icon—he scowls out from the cover in a fuzzy image, as though he was vibrating too energetically for the camera lens to capture. *Blonde on Blonde* confronted record-buyers in 1966 with the first double-LP set in rock, and when stylus met vinyl listeners soon found Dylan no longer offered the doses of acoustic balm that had assuaged the electrified and jangled nerves of earlier recordings. This was a new sound, created in new circumstances. Dylan had gone down to Nashville to record this set, and the experienced country session players hired to back him found that Dylan was a talent that could not be molded to mellifluous pedal steel and pristine arrangements.

"Rainy Day Women #12 & 35" opens the LP with a lurching clamor, with session players reportedly moved around to play unfamiliar instruments and encouraged to follow the song's central suggestion that "everybody must get stoned." The give-and-take between pharmaceutical

bliss and anxiety are replicated throughout the remainder of *Blonde on Blonde,* from the compressed despair of "Stuck Inside of Mobile with the Memphis Blues Again" to the rushing psychedelic blues of "Leopard-Skin Pill Box Hat." Dylan's harmonica, at times tinny and discordant, is placed at the forefront of the mix to create what Dylan himself called "that wild mercury sound."

At a time when pop music was preoccupied with its evergreen agenda—the glorification of romantic love—Dylan spewed out bitterness and anger toward the women in his songs. While "I Want You" and the epic "Sad-Eyed Lady of the Lowlands" contained devotions and desire, these sentiments were countered by the kiss-offs of "Most Likely You Go Your Way (And I'll Go Mine)" and "One of Us Must Know (Sooner or Later)," and the borderline sexist condescension of "Just Like a Woman." Many Dylan songs of this moment seem like acts of revenge, with the narrator enjoying the luxury of an irrefutable, tuneful last word.

Blonde on Blonde is a solid album that

maintains a unity of sound amid the scattershot surrealism and emotional acridity of the lyrics. At its core is a composition that exceeds the ridiculously high standard of the other tracks, one that has to be included in any discussion of Dylan's greatest songs: "Visions of Johanna." Bittersweet and mournful, "Visions" evokes the streets and apartments of New York life, a metaphysical court where all infinity is judged, and the enigma of the Mona Lisa suffering the "highway blues." The lyrics are flawless, Dylan's singing is infused with the longing and wisdom of his best work, and the performance is crisp and precise. It is a stunning song of the sort that fans return to throughout their lives, much as they would a classic novel or poem.

Dylan would not be heard from for a couple years after this album, and when he returned, his music and sensibility had permanently changed. *Blonde on Blonde* is a culmination of the Dylan-as-megastar phenomenon, a time when Dylan was riding a cycle of touring, recording, and writing that would leave him burned out and in need of personal and artistic reorganization. Dylan himself would later admit that he couldn't remember how he wrote these songs. It's probably no exaggeration to say that for about two years, Dylan drove himself so hard and so wild that his mind flowered with a union between the conscious and unconscious. It's no wonder he couldn't keep up the pace.

These tracks brought an intelligence and emotional sophistication to pop music that blew listeners' minds and daunted those who tried to match them. Here was a songwriter who was capable of turning the love song on its head, and a singer whose belief in his own idiosyncratic voice (one of the two greatest in rock history, along with Elvis) pre-empted and trumped criticism. *Blonde on Blonde* is one of a handful of the greatest works in popular music, and its disconnection from the sounds of its day has ensured its freshness and relevance to this day. It is also at times a disturbing and jarring work—but Dylan was never interested in giving you exactly what he thought you wanted, was he?   Q.S.

Sgt. Pepper's Lonely Hearts Club Band

CAPITOL 1967

John Lennon:
guitar, marimba,
Hammond organ,
percussion, vocals

Paul McCartney:
bass, guitar, Hammond
organ, harpsichord,
piano, vocals

George Harrison:
guitar, harmonica, sitar,
tamboura,
tambourine, vocals

Ringo Starr:
bongos, drums,
harmonica, vocals

George Martin:
horn, organ, piano

**Various Additional
Musicians**

Produced by
George Martin

I was all of seven when I first experienced *Sgt. Pepper's Lonely Hearts Club Band*. It was the early seventies and my father, who was completing his doctorate in education, was working on an assignment involving drug references in pop music. I guess he was comfortable with his findings because as soon as he finished his paper, he handed the album to me complete with his notes scrawled around the printed lyrics.

I was immediately taken with Peter Blake's cover art, carefully examining each face. Who were these people? The only faces I recognized were the Beatles and that was after my father pointed them out to me. The cover was somewhat spooky, which made the experience of studying it even more thrilling.

Musically, the album had a carnival vibe that no kid can resist. From the slowly rising sound of a live audience to that last sustained piano chord, I was entranced. Although as a seven-year-old I was unable to grasp it, the Beatles and George Martin had created a study in both lyrical and musical density and complexity; a masterpiece.

I loved the entire record, but the track that

immediately stood out was "Within You Without You." I heard sounds that I'd not experienced before. Aside from George Harrison's slow, prayer-like delivery, I was drawn in by the tamboura and sitar. The song was "psychedelic," though I was years away from being introduced to the concept. I did, however, understand Harrison's plea, " With our love—we could change the world."

Another of my favorites was "She's Leaving Home," which affects me differently today than when I was younger. As the father of a young son, I wonder what goes through the mind of a parent whose child has run away, how they cope with the guilt and grief. McCartney's musical accompaniment could not have complemented the emotionally charged lyrics better.

"Lucy in the Sky with Diamonds" was another song that I connected with. "Picture yourself in a boat on a river . . ." From the start, Lennon asked listeners to join his trip into a surreal, cartoonish place where "cellophane flowers of yellow and green" grew, and let's not forget that "girl with kaleidoscope eyes." A thinly veiled LSD reference? Perhaps. Lennon always denied it, though I'm sure that he preferred that each listener make up his or her own mind. To a slightly naive child, however, it played like a nursery rhyme.

At the time of recording, the Beatles had matured and entered new phases in their lives. They were starting families, exploring spirituality, and experimenting with drugs. They bid farewell to the pop world with their most mature work yet. In doing so, they helped usher in a new genre of recordings: the concept record. There's a feeling of cohesiveness throughout this album; the songs seem sewn together, literally so in the epic suite that closes the album. It is filled with adult themes that were a reflection of the time.

More than thirty years later this album remains in regular rotation in my home and in my car. And my opinion hasn't changed: It is a great album from start to finish.

Today, I'm working in the music business and my dad is retired after a successful career in public education. My three-year-old son is already a Beatles' fan—*Yellow Submarine* is one of his favorite DVDs. But I'll wait until he's a bit older before introducing him to Sgt. Pepper and his Lonely Hearts Club Band. When I do, however, I'm sure it'll have the same lasting effect that it has had on me.

M.G.

The Beatles (The White Album)

APPLE 1968

John Lennon:
vocals, guitars, piano,
organ, harmonica,
bass, tenor saxophone,
tape loops
Paul McCartney:
vocals, bass, guitars,
piano, organ, recorder,
flugelhorn, drums

George Harrison:
vocals, guitars, bass
Ringo Starr:
drums, percussion,
vocals
Produced by
George Martin

The Beatles didn't split up until 1970, but by the time of *The White Album*'s release, the seeds of their dissolution had already been sown. Over the course of this thirty-song, double-disc set, you can practically hear the personalities within the group pulling apart from one another. Such palpable tension could have produced a discouraging mess; instead, it helped create one of their most enduring albums.

Drawing from a vast catalog of songs written during the band's February 1968 retreat to India with the Maharishi Mahesh Yogi, *The White*

Album took shape over a grueling four-and-a-half months of sessions. The psychedelia of the previous year's *Sgt. Pepper* was gone, replaced by a restless eclecticism, more straightforward but no less ambitious. Blues, doo-wop, swing, folk, heavy metal, country—the Beatles tackled them all, along with a dozen other styles of popular music.

However, it soon became brutally clear that there was no longer enough room in the band to accommodate its members' diverging interests. John, now permanently accompanied by his lover, Yoko Ono, took to working in any studio that Paul wasn't occupying. George felt so undervalued by both Lennon and McCartney that he brought in pal Eric Clapton to play lead guitar on his stirring "While My Guitar Gently Weeps," guessing (correctly) that a respected outsider's presence would make his bandmates behave for once.

Sick of the bad vibes, Ringo temporarily left the group; in his absence, Paul played drums on his own old-time rock 'n' roll raveup "Back in the U.S.S.R." and John's delicate "Dear Prudence." Longtime engineer Geoff Emerick also quit in frustration at the band's testiness, while producer George Martin went on vacation for nearly a month, leaving matters in the hands of his assistant Chris Thomas.

What resulted from all this turmoil was an album that revealed the four Beatles's separate natures, and their inner dimensions, as never before. Lennon mourned his late mother on the fragile "Julia," screamed about suicide on "Yer Blues," told hushed fairytales on "Cry Baby Cry," and indulged in outlandish tape-loop experimentation on "Revolution 9." McCartney didn't plumb the emotional depths like his part-

ner, but his musical facility was astounding; no one else could have written the timeless acoustic anthem "Blackbird," the thirties Hollywood pastiche "Honey Pie," the pseudo-reggae charmer "Ob-La-Di, Ob-La-Da," and the raucous tinnitus-inducer "Helter Skelter." Similarly, only Harrison could have penned both the sublime "Long, Long, Long" and the sardonic "Savoy Truffle." And Starr's first solo composition, "Don't Pass Me By," was as plaintive and self-deprecating as one could expect from the most down-to-earth Beatle.

In vain, George Martin tried to convince his charges that one record was better than two, and for the last thirty-plus years, fans have argued about what would've made the cut if *The White Album* had been a single disc. The debate is nonsensical. For without its doodles ("Wild Honey Pie") and its smarmy in-jokes ("Glass Onion"), it would be a lesser work. As it stands, *The White Album* is sprawling, schizophrenic, excessive, at times inexplicable. But it's those very qualities—coupled with great songs and great performances—that make it a singular achievement, one that no band since has matched. M.R.

Exile on Main Street

That album is a really great portrait of the inside of a man; all of his feelings, and all of his egotism, and all of his blindness. The music is like the force of a man. That's a very sexy album, because it's like manhood personified.   —LIZ PHAIR

To say I have lived with *Exile on Main Street* would be an understatement. Though I have owned—and worn-out, lost, or otherwise donated—seven copies of the album over the years, and though I presently own no less than three (scuffed vinyl, CD, and a crusty old cassette I hope never to lose), I never pass a copy in a record store without thinking, however superfluously, I might buy it yet again. It is, I believe, the single greatest rock record there is. I have woken up to it, fallen asleep to it, seduced a friend's girlfriend to it, rolled weed on the sleeve. I have parceled its songs out on mix tapes to innumerable women who've broken my heart, as well as—most importantly—to one who has not. I've given copies to my father and sister, and once drove a car for a year and a half that had a cassette of it lodged, irremovably, in its tape deck. I *know* this record, in short, and yet I never, ever tire of it. This has nothing to do with being an over-ardent Stones fan and everything to do with the sound of a band at their absolute peak, perhaps at anyone's absolute peak. Forget the tired, prancing millionaires of recent years: This is a record made by lean, pasty Englishmen who've been up for days.

To some extent, the band had been trying to create this sound—an original unAmerican blues—since their inception, and have succeeded only partially in their efforts to replicate it ever since. It is the sound of a band—read, perhaps, civilization—coming together in the act of falling apart: Watts' kickstart drumming, Taylor's shit-hot leads, Richards sounding like his guitar is strung with rusty razor-wire. And Jagger sounding committed for once, instead of foppish or tired.

On the brassy opener, "Rocks Off," then the honking, careening "Rip This Joint," Jagger sounds like he's just shoved his hand into a hive of bees. On sleazy, leering covers of Slim Harpo ("Shake Your Hips") and Robert Johnson ("Stop Breakin' Down") he sounds not so much like he's imitating the blues as that he's parodying them as only one who knows them can. On the magnificent barrage of country-soul stompers ("Sweet Virginia," "Torn and Frayed," and

VIRGIN
1972
Keith Richards:
guitar, vocals
Mick Taylor:
guitar
Charlie Watts:
drums
Bill Wyman:
bass
Mick Jagger:
vocals
B. Keys:
sax
J. Price:
trumpet & trombone
N. Hopkins:
piano
Produced by
Jimmy Miller

"Loving Cup"), he slurs and drawls with such abandon that the room looks crooked even as one listens sober. Then there's the joy of Keith's gooseneck vocal on "Happy," butting up against the whooping, exuberant "Turd on the Run," the truncheon-banging frenzy of "Ventilator Blues," the closet-gospel hollering of "Just Wanna See His Face." Factor in a pair of beautiful ballads ("Shine a Light" and "Let It Loose"), the casino two-step of "Tumblin' Dice," the horn-pumped swagger of "All Down the Line"—even the throwaways on this album are masterpieces of a sort: parts of an immaculate whole consisting, oddly, of trash. There are relatively few great songs here, and yet a whole raft of spectacular performances. Never again would the band sound as cohesive, nor anywhere near as anarchic. The paradoxes are many, but what is indisputable is that the Stones here deliver what rock 'n' roll forever promises: a vital toxicity and a sound powerful enough to wake—or bury—the dead.   M.S.

Who's Next

Who's Next in a lot of ways was a perfect record for the Who. It had humor, it had aggression, it had energy, it had color. And it was beautifully recorded. —PETE TOWNSHEND

This scheme was to spawn Who theater, film, and albums. . . . The magnitude of this ambitious project proved too much to handle, but the fragments were salvaged into rock 'n' roll bliss for tens of millions.

I'm guilty. As ashamed and embarrassed as I am to admit it, up until late last year, I ignored the invaluable musical contributions of the Who. Rather than explore the psychological factors that led me to turn my back on one of the greatest bands of all time, I have decided to share my virginal experience with *Who's Next*.

The catalyst for my education was VH1's Concert for New York, an event that featured dozens of acts performing to benefit the Robin Hood Relief Fund in Manhattan. The legend-studded concert raised $33.1 million, most of which, I am convinced, can be attributed to the electrifying performance delivered by the Who. In the current state of glossy pop and pseudo rap, people are looking for something to hold onto, I am looking for something to hold onto. Rock contin-

13

ues as a fading mirror of itself as it forever weakens in failed duplication. The answer, my friends, is not ahead in the future; it's waiting for rediscovery in the past.

1971's *Who's Next* opens with the sound of synthesizers that still sound state-of-the-art over three decades later. Add in Keith Moon's tight thunder, John Entwhistle's ever-changing bass, Roger Daltrey's blistering vocals, and Pete Townshend's windmill licks, and what you have is, quite possibly, musical perfection: "Baba O' Riley." I only wish I had the opportunity to hear "Baba" and the other tracks back in the early seventies. If they're blowing me out of the water today, I can only imagine the impact they would have had on me as they revolutionized rock radio.

Pete Townshend's sanity has been questioned often, even by his bandmates who had trouble understanding the complex concept behind his *Lifehouse* vision. A virtual media montage, the project was to take place in a fictitious future where a single note held the key to salvation. This scheme was to spawn Who theater, film,

MCA
1971
Roger Daltrey:
vocals
Pete Townshend:
guitars, vocals,
synthesizers
John Entwhistle:
bass
Keith Moon:
drums
Produced by
The Who

and albums, all created as a result of interaction between an audience and the band. The magnitude of this ambitious project proved too much to handle, but the fragments were salvaged into rock 'n' roll bliss for tens of millions.

While *Who's Next* has a flavor for every taste, the remnants of the evacuated Lifehouse project resonate through many of the album's songs, thematically reminding the listener that salvation not only lies within, but is entwined in the creative process of making music as well.

Where has this band been my whole life? Maybe I needed an older brother to show me the way. Perhaps just an open mind and some blind luck. Even with half of the band's original lineup traveling up to the musical ethers, I find myself muttering to myself, "Better late than never." *Who's Next* offers a sound that transcends the decades and can be understood intergalactically. And while the Who continue to try to convince us that "Love Ain't for Keeping," there is no doubt that their music certainly is.

A.G.R.

Blue

14

I think the album Blue *was a real personal album. It felt like, gosh, I know everything about this girl just by listening to that album . . . she's amazing.*

—GWEN STEFANI

I have never gone in for that whole hippie thing; that Woodstock-electric kool aid-poncho-wearing pot-smoking give-peace-a-chance type of thing, and for years, my cultural bigotry extended to my musical tastes. I ignored the work of those artists whom I considered part of the crunchy mafia: Bob Dylan, Joan Baez, Cat Stevens, James Taylor, Stephen Stills—what did their music have to do with me? Then at some point in my twenties I was introduced to *Blue*, recorded by a card-carrying member of that club, Joni Mitchell. I embraced the album immediately; its infectious acoustic guitar riffs, its shamelessly naive lyrics, and Mitchell's candor-filled voice telling me about my life. Right. So no one should be surprised that this Canadian-born folk singer's quiet, introspective album of 1971, which

WARNER BROS.
1971
Joni Mitchell:
composer, keyboards, vocals, guitar, piano
Stephen Stills:
guitar, bass
James Taylor:
guitar, vocals
Sneaky Pete Kleinow:
steel guitar, guitar, pedal steel
Russ Kunkel:
drums
Produced by
Joni Mitchell

is both of its time, and transcends it, has emerged as a classic.

When *Blue* was released, Mitchell had already asserted herself as something of a folk diva, with David Crosby producing her debut effort. She was twenty-eight and traveling around Europe when she wrote much of the album, and the content reflects what one might expect of a creative

Like the music itself, Mitchell's lyrics speak volumes with a few poetic, haiku-like strokes. "My Old Man" sums up longing with pictures of a bed and a frying pan that are too big in her lover's absence.

effort forged under such circumstances. Mitchell writes of solitude, love, fleeting associations, heartbreak, exotic adventures, displacement, and missing home.

These were not new ideas or themes. But as a woman who was old enough to know something, Mitchell etched out ten sparse, elegant, and breathtakingly honest tracks that asserted the voice of a commanding and independent female artist.

One of the triumphs of *Blue* is its simplicity. In its original packaging, the record was a monochromatic wash, with a blurred close-up of its author's face drenched in the hue of the album's title gracing the cover, and an inside sleeve color-coordinated to match. (It should be noted that the color blue makes an appearance on over half of the album's songs in various forms: the shade of a friend's eye's, that all-too familiar emotional state, the lonely glow from a TV, a term of endearment.) Most tracks are dominated by one of two instruments—a piano or a guitar—that back Mitchell's liquid, intimate vocals soaring frequently to a moving and confessional falsetto.

Like the music itself, Mitchell's lyrics speak volumes with a few poetic, haiku-like strokes. "My Old Man" sums up longing with pictures of a bed and a frying pan that are too big in her lover's absence. Her adventures on the road are chronicled in songs such as "Carey" and "California," with images of beach tar stuck to the soles of Mitchell's feet, fancy French cologne, and a thieving redneck on a Grecian isle.

Mitchell's lyrics tackle the album's most pervasive theme, love and its many faces, with stunningly economical and endearing phrases. On "All I Want," she expresses the tenderness of the emotion, saying "I want to talk to you, I want to shampoo you," while on "A Case of You," she declares "I could drink a case of you and still be on my feet." Meanwhile, "My Old Man" confesses innocent sentiments of adoration with "He's my sunshine in the morning, he's my fireworks at the end of the day." Mitchell brings this same concentrated eloquence to the task of writing about the loss of love as well. On "River," she plays against the familiar festive melody of "Jingle Bells," singing, "I'm selfish and I'm sad, now I've gone and lost the best baby that I ever had." On "This Flight Tonight," with a driving rhythm guitar mimicking the forward motion of the plane she's on, she pleads "Turn this crazy

bird around. I shouldn't have gotten on this flight tonight."

Yes, this album has the hallmark of a work from the early seventies. It was made in an era of political awareness during which America, and its denizens, were struggling with their identity. But as even the most casual sampling of *Blue* indicates, it would appear that Mitchell was doing

> *Mitchell's lyrics tackle the album's most pervasive theme, love and its many faces, with stunningly economical and endearing phrases.*

the same. No doubt, the album's universal themes are why you can meet people whose copies of *Blue* are a testament to the recording industry's technological advancements, and by default, the album's longevity: They own it on LP, on cassette, and on CD. And you can bet, someone, somewhere, is listening to *Blue* as a series of MP3 files, further proving that some things, like *Blue*, are evergreen. M.O.

The Joshua Tree

ISLAND
1987
Bono:
vocals, harmonica
The Edge:
guitar,
background vocals
Adam Clayton:
bass
Larry Mullen, Jr.:
drums
Produced by
Daniel Lanois
and Brian Eno

I'd been nervously waiting in my bedroom all day for 7 P.M. It was March 4, 1987, and WBCN-Boston had promised to deliver the new U2 single at that time. I was nervous because U2 was my favorite band and I was unsure of the direction they would be taking. There was no Internet then and the band had been tight-lipped about the new material. *The Unforgettable Fire* was a solid effort and the echoes of "MLK," "Pride," and the title track were still churning through my mind.

Finally, with great ceremony, the DJ announced the premiere of "With or Without You." Adam Clayton's haunting bass line emanated dreamily from the speakers and I was immediately hypnotized. I was just nineteen, recently in love for the first or second time, so the lyrics grabbed my attention straight away. "Slight of hand and twist of fate / on a bed of nails she makes me wait." I was mesmerized. I wasn't ready for a love song. I'd been expecting another stab at war, religion, or politics.

Upon release, *The Joshua Tree* was in my possession. It would have been an instant-classic EP if only they'd released the first three songs:

15

"Where the Streets Have No Name," "I Still Haven't Found What I'm Looking For," and "With or Without You." I was stuck on that trio for many months, not ready for the rest of the record, afraid it might be a letdown in the face of these masterpieces. Eventually I was at the record store buying the cassingles to check out the B-sides; pearls like "Silver and Gold," and the cover of Patti Smith's "Dancing Barefoot," soon became shredded ribbons in my very-used Toyota's stereo cassette player.

Christmas that year brought me a CD player and a gift certificate to a record store where I immediately acquired *The Joshua Tree* on compact disc. No more fast-forwarding and rewinding. It was a rediscovery. "One Tree Hill," "Exit," and "Running to Stand Still" became the constant tunes set on my new toy, thanks to the programming feature and infinite repeat. That trilogy was the new heart of the album. I

> *That trilogy was the new heart of the album. I was thinking, "Six songs down, can there be more?" There was. In time, I'd come to digest them all. There isn't a weak link in the chain.*

was thinking, "Six songs down, can there be more?" There was. In time, I'd come to digest them all. There isn't a weak link in the chain.

One night in 1996, I was staying with some friends in their Brooklyn apartment. We'd been trading bong hits when someone came up with a list game comprising our individual top twenty-five albums of all time. Number four I proclaimed was *The Joshua Tree*. One of my buddies shouted, "What are you, nuts? *Joshua Tree* over *Achtung?*"

I didn't back down. *Achtung Baby* was in my top ten and still is today. In fact, I have personally debated which is U2's greatest effort, and I still stand with *The Joshua Tree*.

Today, U2's entire catalog sits on my shelves. I always reach for *The Joshua Tree* first and head right to track nine. At the Foxboro, Massachusetts, stop of *The Joshua Tree* tour, U2 gifted me with the first and only live performance of this track. Check it out.   D . P . G .

Rumours

BURBANK, HOME OF WARNER BROS. RECORDS

RUMOURS
FLEETWOOD MAC
PRODUCED BY FLEETWOOD MAC
with Richard Dashut & Ken Caillat
Engineered by Ken Caillat & Richard Dashut.
Assisted by Cris Morris

1. SECOND HAND NEWS   2:43
(Lindsey Buckingham) Gentoo Music, Inc./Now
Sound Music-BMI

BSK 3010   **SIDE I**

2. DREAMS   4:14
(Stevie Nicks) Gentoo Music, Inc./Welsh Witch
Music-BMI
3. NEVER GOING BACK AGAIN   2:02
(Lindsey Buckingham) Gentoo Music, Inc./Now
Sound Music-BMI
4. DON'T STOP   3:11
(Christine McVie) Gentoo Music, Inc.-BMI
5. GO YOUR OWN WAY   3:38
(Lindsey Buckingham) Gentoo Music, Inc./Now
Sound Music-BMI
6. SONGBIRD   3:20
(Christine McVie) Gentoo Music, Inc.-BMI

All musical compositions administered
by Screen Gems-EMI Music Inc.-
BMI for U.S. & Canada

℗1977 Warner Bros
Records Inc.
3300 Warner Blvd., Burbank Calif. 91505

Warner Bros Records Inc. - a subsidiary and licensee of Warner Bros Inc.

A Warner Communications Company - Made in U.S.A.

WARNER BROS.
1977

**Lindsey
Buckingham:**
guitar, vocals
Stevie Nicks:
vocals
Christine McVie:
keyboards,
synthesizers,
vocals
John McVie:
bass

Mick Fleetwood:
drums,
percussion
Produced by
Fleetwood Mac
with
Richard Dashut
and Ken Caillat

---

*. . . if it weren't for the
eleven songs on* Rumours,
*unforgettable rock and
pop classics all, it would
surely have fallen victim
to its own story.*

If this book were titled *The 100 Greatest Stories About the Greatest Albums of Rock and Roll*, certainly Fleetwood Mac's *Rumours* would have come in at number one. Not that the other albums in these pages don't have great stories—all of them do. But few of them are in any danger of being overshadowed by the behind-the-scenes insanity and melodrama involved in their respective creations. In fact, if it weren't for the eleven songs on *Rumours*, unforgettable rock and pop classics all, it would surely have fallen victim to its own story.

16

Rumours, in part, documents the slow, painful breakups of the two romantic relationships in the band: that of the McVies, John and Christine, as well as Lindsey Buckingham and Stevie Nicks. During recording Nicks started seeing, of all people, Mick Fleetwood. Fleetwood's marriage had been on the rocks for some time after his wife had an affair with former bandmate Bob Weston years earlier. That's only the tip of the iceberg. More sordid details are expanded upon in many places, including—excuse the gratuitous plug—VH1's episode of *Behind the Music: Fleetwood Mac.*

It's a story so riveting, so intimate, you won't feel guilty for being interested in it. The music, however, tells a different story altogether. Three wonderful and distinct singer/songwriters, voices backed by one of the greatest—and perhaps one of the most underrated—rhythm sections in popular music. Nothing to feel guilty about there. The album dominated pop and rock radio with Buckingham's acerbic "Go Your Own Way," Nicks' melancholy "Dreams" (the band's only number one hit single in the U.S.) and Christine McVie's mellow but funky "Don't Stop" and "You Make Loving Fun." "The Chain," not a hit single at the time, is still often heard on the radio, and has gone on to become something of an anthem for the ever-evolving band. "The Chain" is testament to the fact that the lesser-known songs are just as great as the hits. Buckingham's "Second Hand News" which kicks off *Rumours* sets the mood for the album in the first two lines: "I know there's nothing to say/Someone has taken my place." McVie's "Songbird," coming smack in the middle of the record, was a heartbreaking tale of someone in denial about a relationship's end. It became a signature song for her, closing many Mac concerts in the years to come. "Gold Dust Woman," a staple of Mac concerts, as well as Stevie Nicks' solo shows, has been covered by everyone from Waylon Jennings to Hole. The lyrics "Lousy lovers pick their prey/But they never cry out loud" tells the story. They may not "cry out loud," but they do sing beautifully. And while some might be interested in the details of those "lousy lovers," the music here is more than enough.   B.I.

Never Mind the Bollocks

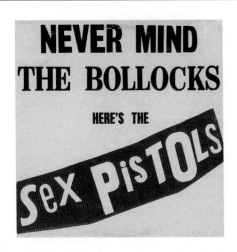

It is a fantastic album. Every song is a little gem, a nasty little gem of balled-up anger, and it's fantastic. It's got so much spitting energy in it. I love it. —SIMON LEBON

No other band managed such a colossal reputation on the basis of such a brief résumé.

They were on the vanguard of hype and image in the innocent days before MTV, a shot of strychnine for a tottering empire, and pure carriers of malice and menace the likes of which had never been imagined. In between publicity stunts, fending off attacks, and various acts of self-destruction, they managed to record one proper album. No other band managed such a colossal reputation on the basis of such a brief résumé.

But what an amazing record it is. *Never Mind the Bollocks* collects the handful of great Sex Pistols singles, recorded on the fly amid U.K. tabloid vilification and a self-created air of apocalyptic meltdown. The great songs on the album—none more than a few minutes long and built from the bricks of the most rudimentary riffs—are twisted psychodramas that rush headlong into the frontier of working-class young-man rage with an intensity that no other band could capture.

Here's the Sex Pistols

17

The key, of course, was Johnny Rotten. Skinny, spotty, acerbic, and self-consciously repugnant, he was also deeply bright, funny, and so disgusted with the world that he allowed no nonsense of any sort to taint the purity of his guerrilla operation. He had never sung before the Sex Pistols, yet his nasal sarcastic whine immediately became one of the most unforgettable tones in rock.

And his lyrics—direct, blunt, biting—were like antisocial haikus that shone the spotlight of Rotten's scorn out, out, out, accusing, denouncing. "Holidays in the Sun," in a few lines, took scattershot aim at Third World tourism, the legacy of the Holocaust (World War II, remember, was little more than two decades past), and England's foundering economy. "God Save the Queen" shocked the U.K. by declaring that its monarch "ain't no human being," and "Anarchy in the U.K." evoked nothing less than total destruction of the social order. In a moment when rock has become a corporate product, sold in the same manner as any other commodity, it

WARNER BROS.
1977
Johnny Rotten:
vocals
Steve Jones:
guitar
Sid Vicious:
bass
Paul Cook:
drums
Produced by
Chris Thomas,
Bill Price

has become difficult to imagine music of such iconoclastic fervor rising up the charts and becoming the stuff of national debate— only some strains of hip-hop come close.

Lest we forget, it also sounded great. The production was minimal, the playing was primitive, the result was impossibly catchy and exciting. Much of the credit goes to Rotten, but Steve Jones's raunch-guitar swagger was essential to the band's amphetamine din. Aside from the Pistols's political material, they also perfected one of rock's great subgenres: the anthem of sneering indolence. "No Feelings," "Liar," and "Pretty Vacant" all portrayed Britain's youth as numbed and hollowed out by hypocrisy and lack of opportunity, offering nothing by way of consolation but a blast of guitar and a keening snarl.

The Sex Pistols were great, then gone. At least they were spared the indignity of trying to follow up on the perfection of their debut. And, for enough cash, they will still come and play the old songs. It has become their final revenge.   Q.S.

Purple Rain

18

The songs are thematically so different from each other and stylistically so different from each other but there is a wonderful cohesion.

—MOBY

I recently picked up a man in a strip club. Never mind why I was there; it was completely innocent, I assure you. That night, suggestive, contemporary hits of the day played over the sound system as half-naked women in a room filled with poles, mirrors, hosts in expensive suits, and champagne attempted to raise the temperature a few degrees. It was sexual, but not surprisingly, it was not sexy.

And then, at some point in the evening, Prince's "Darling Nikki" came over the loudspeaker, and in all its screaming, grunge, percussive, Minneapolis glory, saluting masturbation, intense sex, and seduction, it sent the room back to 1984 to get funky. It was the sexiest song of the

WARNER BROS.
1984
Prince:
bass, guitar, keyboards, vocals
Apollonia:
vocals
Bobby Z:
drums, percussion
Brownmark:
bass, vocals
Lisa Coleman:
keyboards, sitar, vocals
Matt Fink:
keyboards, vocals
Suzie Katayama:
viola, violin
Wendy Melvoin:
guitar, percussion, vocals
Novi Novog:
cello
Produced by
Prince, David Coleman

night. I started making out with the guy who had been sitting next to me. Needless to say, I took him home.

Can someone just say it, already? We are blessed to be living in the presence of a few geniuses; among them are Nelson Mandela, Paul McCartney, Mick Jagger—

Forgive him for pretentiously turning his name into a symbol; genius has its price, identity complexes apparently included.

and Prince. Prince, who released his first album at the age of twenty, who might rightly, by the enlightened, be thought of as the Mozart of our time. Forgive him for pretentiously turning his name into a symbol; genius has its price, identity complexes apparently included. As an average Joe, you have your Braun coffeemaker, your Panasonic VCR, the magnets on the refrigerator that you compose into poetic little phrases for your wife. Prince, whoever he is, has his catalog. And while he may not have a neatly arranged photo

album, if he did, part of that pictorial would be images from the year he took the world by storm in 1984 with the album known as *Purple Rain.*

Yes, it was a cheesy, unbearable, trite, and overtly sexual movie with some of the worst dialogue ever committed to celluloid, but the soundtrack, and the tour it produced, were a gift. This is not an album that was missed by popular culture. With the help of a young singer named Madonna who was on the rise at the time, Purple Rain and its aesthetic infused our culture with a lace-trimmed, sexed-up, baroque, and orgasmically breathy over-the-top sensibility. There were many hits. "When Doves Cry," "Purple Rain," "Let's Go Crazy," and "I Would Die 4 U" all topped the charts throughout the year. At one point, the then twenty-six-year-old claimed the number-one spot on *Billboard*'s single and album charts, while also occupying the number-one position at the box office with his film. *Purple Rain* spent a stunning twenty-four weeks as the most popular album in the country, and come Oscar time, Prince sauntered away with the statue for Best Score.

In some ways, this is an album cursed by its hits, denying many the pleasure of listening to it from start to finish. Purple Rain's songs infiltrated the Top 40, roller rinks, and your best friend's bedroom. You almost didn't have to buy the album because it was everywhere—but many of us did. We held on to it, deciding once and again to forgo throwing it out, selling it, or giving it away, regardless of the medium on which we owned it (i.e., tape, or God forbid, even vinyl). Why? Because beyond being a reminder of simpler days, it's just so damn good.

To literally look at the album now, *Purple Rain* is hopelessly dated. The fonts that cover the lyric sheet, liner notes, and back cover represent a catalog of inelegant, almost crass typefaces that our media-savvy eyes are long immune to, ripped from even the slightest sophisticated greeting card program. But the songs, which speak of "Dr. Everything Will Be All Right" ("Let's Go Crazy"), ask the question, "Where is my love life? Where can it be?" ("Computer Blue"), bizarrely explain, "I'm not a woman, I'm not a man" ("I Would Die For U"), and

Yes, it was a cheesy, unbearable, trite, and overtly sexual movie with some of the worst dialogue ever committed to celluloid, but the soundtrack, and the tour it produced, were a gift.

screamingly plead, "Do you want him or do you want me—'cause I want you" ("The Beautiful Ones") are truly timeless.

When one lives among a genius, it is a tough call as to who we would like to see go first. Regardless of whenever any of us meet their maker, there is one thing we should all go to our graves thinking, with Prince in mind, as we are lucky to have the chance to witness him do his thing: Thank U 4 a funky time. Call us up whenever U want 2 grind.   M.O.

The Velvet Underground and Nico

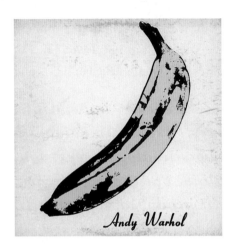

It was so ahead of its time. While everyone was doing psychedelic, they were doing nasty, grungy songs.

—FRED SCHNEIDER

I cannot rightly remember where I was upon first hearing *The Velvet Underground and Nico.* Not because the event was unmemorable—on the contrary—but because the record was so startling, so utterly evocative of a time and place not my own (a real, or mythological, New York of the late sixties), it fairly annihilated everything around me. It must have been in my adolescent bedroom—I do not recall sharing an interest in the Velvet Underground with any-one, in Los Angeles in the early eighties (though there *must* have been others interested at that time, since every significant local band, the Dream Syndicate and other members of the so-called "Paisley Underground," were trans-parently indebted. So too, all the cool bands from England, the Smiths, the Jesus and Mary Chain, and so on.)

But I think I was alone, as I felt alone, and as I still feel alone hearing the record to this day. It is a rivening kind of loneliness the record evokes, that is its secret theme: the deceptively gentle "Sunday Morning," which opens the record, is about stumbling home on one's own after an extended night out. Followed by the pounding, propulsive "I'm Waiting for the Man," with its weird, discordant piano and its lyric about scoring drugs in a strange neighborhood. This record *was* that neighborhood to me, and while its blank-faced nihilism has come to seem more cartoonish than creepy (as in the grinding, viola-led S&M ode, "Venus In Furs," and the famous, whisper-to-a-screech junkie proclamation "Heroin"), the songs themselves have lost nothing of their original enigmatic charm. If "charm" is the right word for a record as hostile, as defiantly (and sometimes pretentiously) avant-garde as this one: to wit, the indecipherable "The Black Angel's Death Song," or the concluding "European Son" (dedicated to Lou Reed's friend and mentor, the poet Delmore Schwartz), which includes the sound of metal chairs being thrown around the studio. But then there is also the lulled beauty of "I'll Be Your Mirror" and "Femme Fatale," the modal

UNI/A&M
1967
Lou Reed:
guitar, keyboards, vocals
John Cale:
bass, keyboards, piano, viola
Sterling Morrison:
bass, guitar
Maureen Tucker:
bass, drums, percussion
Nico:
chant, vocals

Produced by
Tom Wilson
and Andy Warhol

wonder of "All Tomorrow's Parties," and—lest you get the idea it's all about droning violas and Warhol-inspired posturing—the hip-shaking riff of "There She Goes Again," nicked from Marvin Gaye's "Hitchhike." And even the record's most turbulent instances, the circular melody (or near-melody) of "The Black Angel's Death Song," the squealing feedback that ends "Heroin," which sounds like subway brakes and is, in its way, the record's defining moment, retain both a thrilling, rockin' primitivism as well as a forward-looking, form-shattering originality.

The Velvets would go on to make records both more punishing (the stunning, hyper-amplified *White Light White Heat*) and—after losing both John Cale's viola and Nico's affectless, perfectly matched vocals—more beautiful (the limpid, exquisite *The Velvet Underground*), this album, the band's first, remains the definitive article, as transporting today as it was when I first heard it.　　　　M.S.

It Takes a Nation of Millions

DEF JAM 1988

Chuck D:
vocals

Flava Flav:
vocals

Terminator X:
turntables

Professor Griff:
Minister of
Information

**Hank Shocklee,
Carl Ryder:**
producers

**Eric (Vietnam)
Sadler:**
assistant producer

Rick Rubin:
executive producer

Bill Stephney:
production
supervisor

It Takes a Nation of Millions to Hold Us Back is one of the most influential hip-hop albums of all time. But few—if any—hip-hop albums ever had such a huge influence over rock music. By the late eighties, Run-D.M.C. and LL Cool J had enough crossover appeal to take hip-hop to the suburbs, but the hip-hop they were bringing was, for the most part, party music. Public Enemy were angry. While their music was certainly funky, Chuck D's vocals and lyrics were dead serious. Like punk rock from a different part of town.

Nation was both lyrically and sonically radical. It had an explosive, aggressive sound that was totally unique at the time, and which influenced artists as diverse as Sonic Youth, Anthrax, Beastie Boys, Red Hot Chili Peppers, and The Chemical Brothers. Meanwhile, Chuck D's lyrics rattled the establishment ("Farrashan's a prophet and I think you out to listen to what he can say to you, what you ought to do.") and educated white kids about the reality of the black experience. By the late eighties, there weren't too many figures left in popular music that could genuinely scare a generation of parents who were largely brought up during the original rock 'n' roll era. So here was a band with a new sound, *and* who were threatening to Mom and Dad to boot.

Public Enemy's secret weapon was the dichotomy within the group: Chuck D, the "Hard Rhymer," was a master at bringing the hard truths to the table. Flavor Flav, the "Cold Lamper," provided comic relief. While Chuck was being dead serious, Flav would lighten the mood. Each MC prevented the music from getting either too message-oriented or too zany. The combination of Chuck, Flav, and the innovative music allowed fans to, as the last song on the album recommended, "Party for Your Right to Fight." No group in any genre has ever come close to Public Enemy's unique yin-and-yang chemistry.

Great chemistry leads to good albums. Great lyrics are often (but not always) found on good albums. Innovative sounds can be the hallmark of a good album. But *classic* albums are classic because of the songs. And *It Takes a Nation...* is filled with classic songs. The album kicks off with "Countdown to Armageddon." Recorded live in the U.K., this is Chuck's statement that hip-hop had finally gone global. Then straight into "Bring the Noise," a mission statement, not just for themselves, but for hip-hop in general, a throwing down of the gauntlet against those who criticized it. The album goes on to attack the media ("Don't Believe the Hype"), the government ("Louder Than a Bomb"), black radio stations that wouldn't play their music ("Hype," "Caught, Can I Get a Witness?," "Rebel Without a Pause"), empty-minded television ("She Watch Channel Zero?!"), and drugs ("Night of the Living Baseheads"). Elsewhere, the spotlight was aimed at Flav ("Flavor Flav Cold Lampin'") and Terminator X ("Terminator X to the Edge of Panic"). "Black Steel in the Hour of Chaos" is a chilling tale of a prison breakout, which, in lesser hands, would come off as a bad B-movie. Instead, it is an utterly authentic and gripping narrative that showed Chuck D to be a storyteller on par with Bruce Springsteen, Johnny Cash, and Stevie Wonder.

It Takes a Nation... is more than just a classic album. It did for hip-hop what the Beatles did for rock 'n' roll: It elevated the genre to an art form.   B . I .

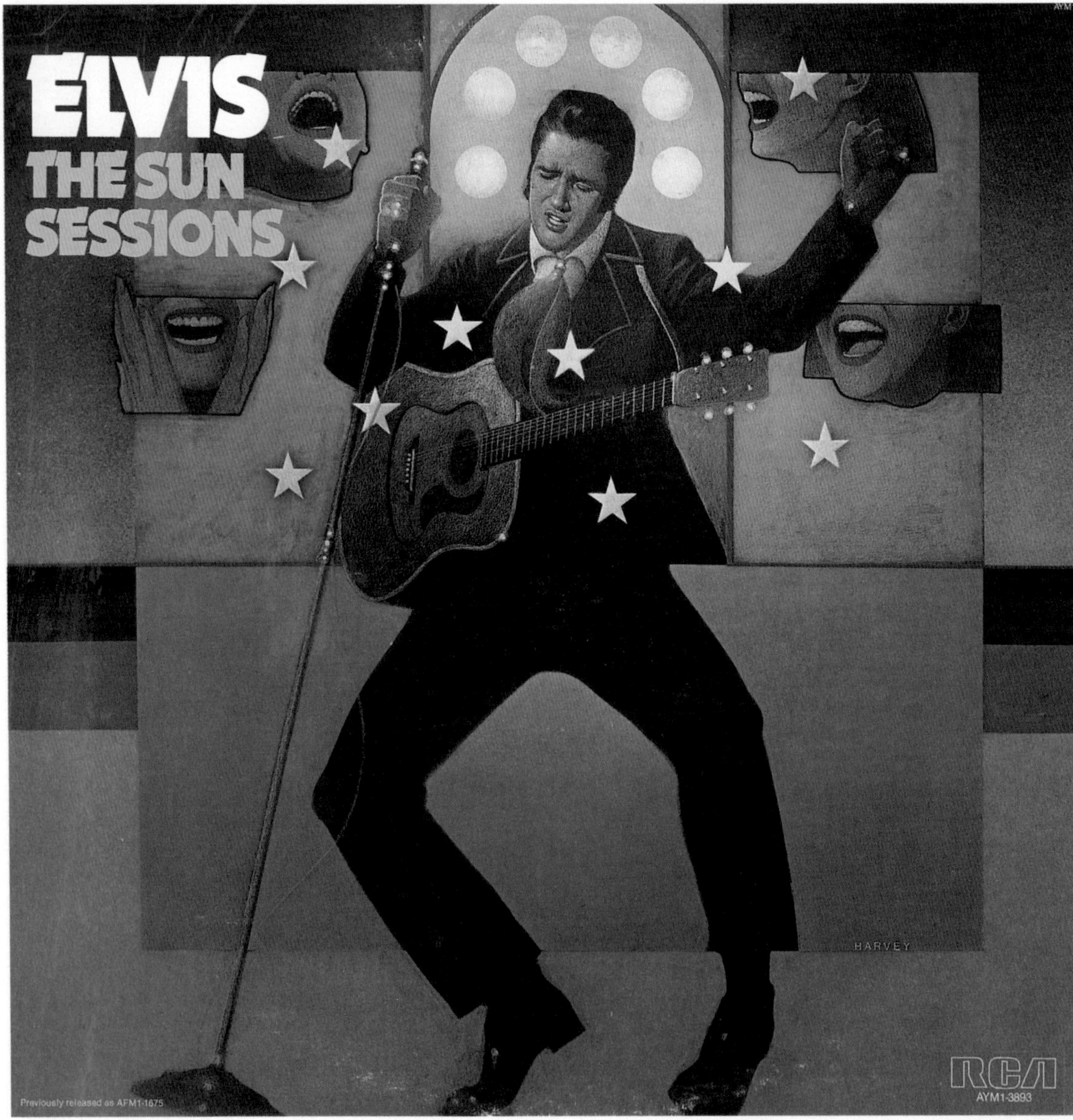
ELVIS
THE SUN
SESSIONS
HARVEY
Previously released as AFM1-1675
RCA
AYM1-3893

The Sun Sessions

21

One of the unfortunate factors of the first half of the twentieth century was the spotty recording legacy of some of its most important musical practitioners. Before the advent of the LP record in the mid-fifties, the majority of recordings were done in either 78 or, later, 45 RPM form, which usually meant a maximum of two songs per disc. Add to that the volatile nature of some of the century's musical giants—like Robert Johnson or Charlie Parker, for instance—and it's clear that sometimes the greatest recordings of the era didn't even see the light of day until many years later. In the case of *The Sun Sessions*, there's little doubt that the sounds here provided the ignition for the entire rock revolution. But it was only after Elvis had switched to RCA, become famous, and begun recording more pop-oriented material that these recordings were finally given the respect they deserved.

Initially, when Colonel Tom Parker had wooed Elvis away from Sam Phillips, part of the deal was that RCA

RCA
1975 (recordings
made 1954–55)

Elvis Presley:
vocals, guitar

Scotty Moore:
guitar

Bill Black:
bass

DJ Fontana:
drums

Produced by
Sam Phillips

9189
Columbia

BOB DYLAN HIGHWAY 61 REVISITED

Highway 61 Revisited

22

The following is an edited transcript of an online conversation that took place on a late December night in 2002 between five members of the Dylan scholarly collective and pirate radio station known as WBOB. The group convened at VH1's request to discuss Bob Dylan's *Highway 61 Revisited*, its place in the Dylan canon, and in rock and roll.

HANDYDANDY: you got the album playin?

JOKERMAN: no, we can't find it. what else is new?

HANDYDANDY: i have to listen to the greatest hits, forgot 61 at work.

JOKERMAN: here it is.

GUILTYUNDERTAKER: we all know the songs.

HANDYDANDY: they'll stone you when you're tryin to make a book.

WBOB101: does anyone here rate this dylan's best album?

GUILTYUNDERTAKER: not me.

WBOB101: i for one, don't. well, not necessarily . . .

JOKERMAN: If its not his best it is definitely top three.

HANDYDANDY: i think it's the definitive sixties dylan album.

RUEMORGUEAVENUE: one of his masterpieces.

WBOB101: always loved this album's diversity. it's got everything. right now listening to "it takes a lot to laugh, it

---

COLUMBIA
1965

Bob Dylan:
vocals, guitar, harmonica

Mike Bloomfield:
guitar

Alan Kooper:
organ, piano

Paul Griffin:
piano, organ

Bobby Gregg:
drums

Harvey Goldstein:
bass

Charley McCoy:
guitar

Frank Owens:
piano

Russ Savakus:
bass

Produced by
Bob Johnston,

**except "(Like a)
Rolling Stone," which
was produced by**
Tom Wilson

takes a train to cry." it's so easy. so is "desolation row," though trippier . . . then there are all the uptight "ballad of a thin man" tunes. and "like a rolling stone," the ultimate sixties rock tune.

GUILTYUNDERTAKER: the ultimate rock song period.

HANDYDANDY: i don't know if the album is as perfect as *john wesley harding* or as far out as *blonde on blonde,* but it's the culmination of the records before it and sets the stage for everything after.

GUILTYUNDERTAKER: indeed.

RUEMORGUEAVENUE: but back to Highway 61 as I listen to "It Takes a lot . . ."

HANDYDANDY: i've really been diggin that song lately.

WBOB101: oh yeah. "takes a lot" is a masterpiece. a real *song* song, not just a dylan song. i imagine it's a near straight-up cop, though, of an older blues tune.

HANDYDANDY: all blues tunes are cops of blues tunes.

WBOB101: sure, but you know.

HANDYDANDY: dylan knows the blues.

WBOB101: yes he does.

JOKERMAN: How about the album cover?

HANDYDANDY: yeah, what do you make of that?

WBOB101: sick. a new standard of cool.

HANDYDANDY: i was trying to make sense of his face.

JOKERMAN: Its almost a James Dean look with the slightly menacing look and the motorcycle t-shirt

WBOB101: it's like, "aw come on now, you're not gonna tell me that shit, are you?"

JOKERMAN: He has definitely left his mythical backwoods period for a street kind of thing.

WBOB101: the camera, and the bold colors and the triumph shirt (especially given the motorcycle accident), the cropping . . . it's all fantastic, even the type.

HANDYDANDY: i think it was on this album that he redefined the rock star.

WBOB101: yeah, a strain of rock star, definitely.

HANDYDANDY: you don't get to jim morrison, the beatles don't go psychedelic . . .

WBOB101: huh?

HANDYDANDY: elvis doesn't come back in 69 . . .

WBOB101: ha ha

HANDYDANDY: without dylan going full on into rock

HANDYDANDY: did you dig this record as soon as you heard it?

JOKERMAN: well "Rolling Stone" had a ton of air-time which drew Dylan fans and others to the album. The most compelling thing about the album is that its words and music were totally unique for the time. Nobody had heard an album like that before. how about the band?

WBOB101: superb band

JOKERMAN: Bloomfield's guitar sizzles

HANDYDANDY: the guitar licks are constant and yet never a solo. you can tell the band is having fun, but they always seem to be hanging by a thread. there's a lot of tension in the transitions. you don't get that with many other bands.

WBOB101: just about every dylan band, tho.

HANDYDANDY: yeah, but it all starts here on this album. he used bands behind him before, but they just sounded like they were playing behind the singer. this really feels like a band.

WBOB101: i would guess "desolation row" blew some minds at the time, huh?

RUEMORGUEAVENUE: yes it did, it was the only acoustic number on the album.

GUILTYUNDERTAKER: odd, too, in that it ends the record.

WBOB101: you can really hear dylan bobbing and weaving closer and farther from the mic in "desolation."

HANDYDANDY: dylan's always gone with the live setting in the studio and he likes to sing and play simultaneously. he's never gone for that clean production. better to get the essence of the song, the energy, than refine it into blandness.

WBOB101: wow. this is the first time i've listened to that tune on my new stereo and i am hearing some freaky shit at the end.

HANDYDANDY: "desolation row" gave birth to bruce springsteen

WBOB101: may have given birth to bowie too

RUEMORGUEAVENUE: well, lots of people are bound to pick up something

HANDYDANDY: dylan gave birth to all of them, really

WBOB101: it's true—they all kind of look like him, too. you ever notice?

HANDYDANDY: especially that kid in the wallflowers

WBOB101: no, that's bloomfield's son

HANDYDANDY: any last thoughts?

JOKERMAN: If God came and said you can keep one Dylan album it might just be *Highway 61* although *Blonde* has more songs

RUEMORGUEAVENUE: nobody mentioned "Tombstone"

JOKERMAN: one of the greatest songs for listening to the band. and what a comment on society. things haven't gotten any better since 1966. in fact, they've gotten worse.

WBOB101: story of america.

HANDYDANDY: dylan's always been able to do that.

WBOB101: is there a hole for me to get sick in?

HANDYDANDY: the sun's not yellow it's chicken

WBOB: *All Bob, All The Time*

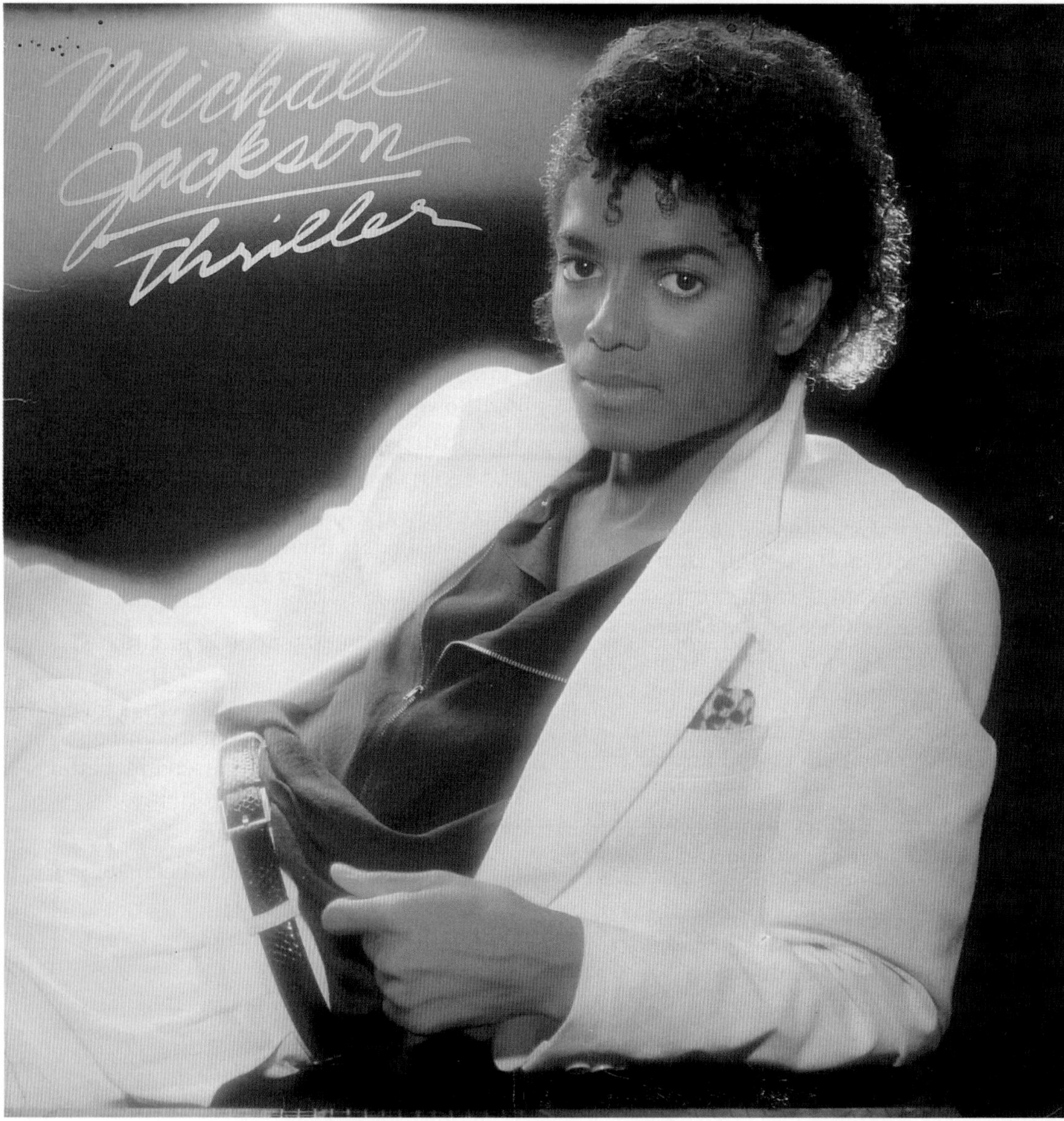
Michael Jackson
Thriller

Thriller

23

Let's just get this out of the way: *Thriller* is the best-selling record of all time. If God were to record a compendium of catchy pop tunes, it is unclear as to whether the sales could compete. At last count, *Thriller* had sold 46 million copies, and although it's hard to believe, there are still some people in the world who do not own this album, which only means that this astronomical number will continue to grow. In the year of *Thriller*'s release, Michael Jackson was twenty-three, and the album, a collaboration with friend and veteran producer Quincy Jones, was a follow-up to the singer's impressive but hardly record-shattering or prophetic debut effort, *Off the Wall*.

It is truly difficult to view *Thriller* in a vacuum, as a musical offering separate from its context, because the album itself played a part in defining the time of its release. Few people who were sentient beings in the early eighties can hear tracks from the album and not be transported to their past. It is also hard to determine the flash-

> **SONY**
> 1982
> **Michael Jackson:**
> vocals
> **Various musicians**
>
> **Produced by**
> Quincy Jones

point of Michael Mania, a truly innocent phenomenon that rivals the hysteria inspired by the Beatles, but his performance on *Motown 25* in May 1983 is certainly a moment during which many people sat up and took notice. It was then that the formerly adorable boy genius who'd fronted the Jackson 5 showed the signs of being a genius all on his own. The singer unleashed "Billie Jean," and perhaps his most famous dance move, the moonwalk, on an unsuspecting public that night—and the rest, as the self-proclaimed King of Pop might claim, is history. Inspired by Jackson's style—displayed through the videos which irrefutably mandated space for black artists on MTV's airwaves—self-respecting people donned single white gloves and horrifically tacky and expensive red and black leather jackets as seen in the videos for "Thriller" and "Beat It."

Thriller, for all of its furor, is composed of a scant nine tracks—seven of which were Top 10 hits. The album dominated the charts in 1982, occupying the number-one spot for thirty-seven weeks. The record-buying public wasn't the only group who thought *Thriller* was a triumph: Jackson walked away from the Grammys that year with eight statues,

Individually, the songs leap off the album as perfect pop creations. The title track, opening with a delightfully hokey horror movie intro complete with eerie howls, has Jackson insisting "Girl, I could thrill you more than any ghoul could ever dare try." B-horror flick mainstay Vincent Price closes out the song with a cameo voiceover (described on the liner notes as a "rap") and what might be considered the definitive campy maniacal laugh—that echo reverberates for a while.

Price is not the only famous friend to appear on the album: Eddie Van Halen lends a compact, safely dangerous guitar solo to the peace-promoting "Beat It," and "The Girl Is Mine" finds Jackson and Paul McCartney verbally sparring over the affections of what one can only assume is one hell of a woman. In a chummy spoken break of playful rivalry, McCartney informs Jackson he was told he was the woman's "forever lover," while Jackson assures the former Beatle he's "a lover, not a fighter."

Thriller is truly an album of its time: It is wrapped in the rich, synthesizer-laden production that came to be the hallmark of much of the music of the eighties. The recording is so multilayered and techno-infused that at times, it almost shimmers. Beyond that, within the irresistibly catchy universe of *Thriller*, Jackson skillfully traverses many moods. "Billie Jean," with its insistent, ever-present bass line, is probably the only treatment of a paternity accusation to create both a feeling of claustrophobia and the need to tap one's foot. "The Lady in My Life" and the exquisite, expansively mellow "Human Nature" are the album's slow-tempo offerings, with Jackson playing the role of a seductive Romeo, while "Baby Be Mine" and "P.Y.T. (Pretty Young Thing)" are straight-up pop confections that expertly follow the rules of the form—Jackson pleads for the attention of a girl to an addictively upbeat rhythm.

No discussion of *Thriller* would be complete without acknowledging, not what Jackson says, but what he doesn't say on the nine tracks. It was on this album that Jackson cemented his ability to seduce listeners with sounds not used in common conversation: He peppers the recording with undeniably seductive incidental exclamations ("Hoo-hoo," "Hee-hee," "Ow!," etc.), guttural grunts, heavy breathing, hiccups, and at times, pure nonsense. "Diddy-baum" and "Ma ma se, ma ma sa, ma coo sa" are phrases all delivered with commitment on this album, and through Jackson's sublime, inspired delivery, it all works. There's also the lyric from the hit that millions sang along to, "Wanna Be Startin' Somethin,'" that technically, is plain English: "You're a vegetable." What on earth Jackson really means with this line is somewhat elusive, but like the rest of the record, it sounds so good it's hard to really care. At last count, 46 million people are not troubled by this ambiguity, and no doubt in years to come, several more million won't be either. M.O.

Let It Bleed

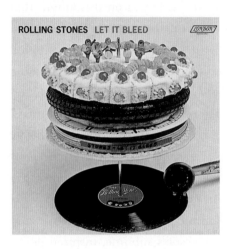

ROLLING STONES LET IT BLEED

I love the Stones and always have. *Let It Bleed* was more influential to me because I just made it a point to learn every song on the record. —ROBIN ZANDER, CHEAP TRICK

"This Record Should Be Played Loud." Sound advice. By this time, the Stones were referring to themselves as "The World's Greatest Rock 'n' Roll Band." *Let It Bleed* is irrefutable evidence to that fact, a bold and aggressive challenge to anyone who might dare to disagree.

The album picked up where *Beggars Banquet* had left off, continuing the Stones' commitment to a bluesy, gritty sensibility following a flirtation with the psychedelic sound of the sixties.

Let It Bleed is the consummate rock 'n' roll album, infused with a sinister, rolicking, and chaotic attitude that channeled both the Stones's decadent image and the tumultuous tenor of the end of the decade.

The record includes all of the hallmarks of classic rock 'n' roll: drugs, sex, and broken hearts. A seedy bar filled with cheap beer and cheap women is the ideal setting in which to enjoy the album as much of it sounds as if it was recorded in a honky-tonk. But for all its raw energy, *Let It Bleed* is hardly an onslaught of noise. Its production is open and loose, allowing even the delicate sounds on the album to shine through.

24

Indeed, moderation is key to the album's success. Tracks such as Robert Johnson's timeless love song "Love in Vain," and "You Got the Silver" offer a subdued but equally powerful counterpoint to the record's in-your-face songs like "Monkey Man" and "Live with Me," in which Mick Jagger declares, "I've got nasty habits."

Almost without exception, the songs on *Let It Bleed* build masterfully to alternately ominous and triumphant climaxes, fueled by relentless, driving guitar, bass, and soulful piano lines. The pleading "Gimme Shelter" is accented by harmonic riffs and howling backup vocals and plays like a sonic freight train barreling down everything in its path. Other songs swell similarly to varying conclusions: "Midnight Rambler," to the final menacing lyric, "I'll stick my knife right down your throat"; the title track finds its end in a spirited and bluesy piano-backed tumble, while the record's sendoff, the anthemic

ABKCO
1969
Mick Jagger:
guitar, harmonica, harp, keyboards, vocals
Brian Jones:
autoharp, guitar, harp, keyboards, percussion, vocals
Keith Richards:
bass, guitar, guitar (acoustic), keyboards, vocals
Leon Russell:
piano
Ian Stewart:
keyboards, piano
Mick Taylor:
guitar, slide guitar, vocals
Charlie Watts:
drums
Bill Wyman:
autoharp, bass, harp, keyboards, synthesizer, vibraphone, vocals
Produced by
Jimmy Miller

"You Can't Always Get What You Want," explodes into a wash of symphonic choir vocals.

Finally, while *Let It Bleed* is without a doubt a product of the unique synergy of the band's members, the performances by the Stones' lead songwriters, Jagger and Richards, are exceptional. Richards's guitar playing on the album, masterful and marked by stunning precision and restraint, would become a cornerstone of the group's signature sound. Jagger, already well on his way to becoming the prototypical rock 'n' roll hellion, unleashes his trademark swagger with full force, sneering and howling, injecting his vocals with seductive and menacing sexuality, venom, and poignant sorrow.

When the Stones dubbed themselves the best band in the world, some may have understandably perceived them as hubristic egomaniacal rock stars. But when you listen to an album like *Let It Bleed*, it's difficult to disagree. M.O.

The Clash

LONDON

CALLING

THIS ALBUM INCLUDES
LYRIC CONTENT WHICH
MAY BE OFFENSIVE TO
SOME MEMBERS
OF THE PUBLIC

London Calling

25

It was 1983 and we were a scaly lot—wildly pimpled and wildly grinning. And, by our own standards, mighty good looking, and ready for anything.

We had been meddling with the other rock that was out there—the Minutemen, X, Fishbone. And of course, the reggae—Black Uhuru, Burning Spear, Peter Tosh, etc. All of us were Bad Brains adherents—whom we regularly saw at the Ritz on Thirteenth Street. Yet none of it, exactly, was music that was ours. We found ourselves on a continuous search for something we hadn't yet heard, and on some level, the music we listened to was the imprecise answer of limited options.

What else was there? The Duran Duran agenda was far too polished for us—and surely, a sound like that was part of the machine we so resented. We were consciously aware, in the shoulder pads and rolled cuffs of the early eighties, that rock 'n' roll had become the preferred entry to conformity. That rebellion had been canned. Billy Joel or Bruce Springsteen had an aura, to us, of the suburban, as did heavy metal. Music, for a teenager, was as much about style as sub-

> EPIC
> 1979
> **Mick Jones:**
> guitars, vocals
> **Joe Strummer:**
> vocals, rhythm guitar
> **Paul Simenon:**
> bass, vocals
> **Topper Headon:**
> drums, percussion
> **Produced by**
> Guy Stevens

stance, and whatever we secretly thought of a song, there was no forgiving long hair, or sympathy for New Jersey (Jerseyites being the arch faux pas to any of us Manhattanites). American, white rock 'n' roll had a distinctly nonurban history. Early on, those first city crooners, singing about life under the boardwalk, had been co-opted by the rural Elvis, and the L.A. garage band, and eventually, after other incarnations, by the Seattle grunge scene. Urban life had become singularly "black." And in fact, many of us listened singularly to rap (many an identity crisis resulting). Anyone with a credible sense of reality, however, knew that our urban experience was not then represented in rap. As for punk—it was just too silly.

When we were first introduced to the Clash, we found the urban heavy metal that we had been craving. Not only did they satisfy our anger but our sense of romanticism about city life—as easily represented in the form of London as New York. As for the musical elements—the punk and reggae—we were well prepped, as we'd been listening to music like that for years. Here was a thinking man's Sex Pistols, or a young, white Bad Brains. Finally, without hair-shaking or safety pins, we could relate: "New York, New York, 42nd Street, / Hustlers rustle and pimps pimp the beat."

Additionally, the Clash's mocking, if emotive attitude toward life extended as far as themselves, and in that, was a perfect counterpoint to the near-universal hypocrisy. The Clash were not ashamed of the fact that they were mournful, drunk, and a little goofy. How could that fail to appeal to us? And yet still, as puny as they were—as puny as we were—the rage felt real: "Like skyscrapers rising up / Floor by floor, I'm not giving up."

Work hard and get ahead—we were overwhelmed not only by our disbelief in the lie, but also by our belief in it. It was America in the fifties, again—although now with a sense of irony. (In the eighties, the fifties really was the decade that we were reliving—from the hamburger to the miniskirt.) And that fifties awkwardness and hint of rockabilly that was so intense to the culture (the Stray Cats, the Fine

Young Cannibals), it was also there in the Clash, but rawer—in songs such as "Brand New Cadillac," "Jimmy Jazz," and "Wrong 'em Boyo." And as for that rebel-without-a-cause, he was also there for us, in songs like "Revolution Rock" and "Rudie Can't Fail," where the reggae influence offered not only a critique of all that was absurd, plain, and sinister, but a personal solution. "Get rude and reckless. Look cool and speckless. Drink brew for breakfast."

The Clash had honed a response to the angst of the time—represented in songs like "Lost in the Supermarket" and "Working for the Clampdown." But the real battle, the Clash had realized, was against our own fantasy of rebellion—that mythic rebellion characterized in "The Guns of Brixton:" "When they kick at your front door / How you gonna come?" Like many, I imagine that teenager in me is still waiting—dreaming of the falling door . . .

The truth is that waiting isn't enough. And however consciously, we all knew that the Clash was singing to the tragedy and legend of our own failure. In the songs, "Death or Glory" and "Four Horsemen," every note played and word sung speaks directly to this awareness of the con—the fraud we were perpetuating on even ourselves. And today, with my generation slowly taking the helm—what do we have? Disco lives on in dance music and rap so sharp and so smooth—and so without tooth. And the pre-rock 'n' roll ballad has returned to the fore in a new rockish format. And even the littile rock 'n' roll that's left is casually tendered as a form of societal initiation. The only comfort that we can take in the death of rock 'n' roll is that most of us probably died right along with it. And the Clash made sense of it all. Basements and streets as dingy as our own optimism. Handclaps and beats as dragging as our own footsteps through the inevitability of our lives. And a music of endless defiance, and endless surrender: "That's just the beat of time—the beat that must go on / If you been trying for years—then we already heard your song."

So *London Calling* is on the greatest albums list. Well, it is a great album—so go buy it! In the end they get us all.   J.R.

Exodus

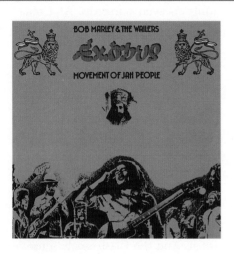

ISLAND RECORDS 1977

Bob Marley:
lead vocal, rhythm
guitar, acoustic
guitar, percussion

**Aston "Familyman"
Barrett:**
Fender bass, guitar,
percussion

Carlton Barrett:
drums, percussion

Tyrone Downie:
keyboards,
percussion,
backing vocals

**Alvin "Seeco"
Patterson:**
percussion

**Julian (Junior)
Marvin:**
lead guitar

**I Threes (Rita
Marley, Marcia
Griffiths, Judy
Mowatt):**
backing vocals

Produced by
Bob Marley &
the Wailers

Never has one artist so completely dominated the public's perception of a genre as Bob Marley. Many people's understanding of reggae comes from a lone copy of his greatest-hits set, *Legend,* which they likely picked up in college. *Exodus* is oftentimes that pivotal second album for those discovering the power and the passion of Bob Marley & the Wailers. Truly a classic, it remains one of the strongest testimonials of Marley's lasting influence and popularity.

After an assassination attempt on his life, Marley fled Jamaica and went to England, where he holed up in Island Records' London studios, fervently writing the tracks that would become *Exodus* and its follow-up, *Kaya.* It was a time of paranoiac turmoil for Marley, who feared further attempts on his life, but also one of great artistic output that resulted in some of his most memorable tunes.

If 1976's *Rastaman Vibration* had been the group's Stateside breakthrough, then *Exodus* truly opened the floodgates. Composed of ten striking originals, with the exception of the closer "One Love/People Get Ready," which owed half its parentage to the great Curtis Mayfield, *Exodus* was a tour de force. Thematically, it is divided by its darker, unrepentant political and religious anthems ("Exodus," "The Heathen") and its moments of uplifting joy and love-struck playfulness ("Three Little Birds," "Waiting In Vain"). Fading up into the slacker skank of "Natural Mystic," Marley promises "I won't tell no lie / If you listen carefully now, you will hear" and then on "So Much Things to Say" he proclaims, "I and I no come to fight flesh and blood / But spiritual wickedness in high and low places." Those two lyrics sum up the underlying intent of *Exodus*—to reveal the universal truths and excise the demons that haunted the world around him. As he sang on "One Love/People Get Ready," it was as simple as "One love, one heart / Let's get together and feel all right."

Sometimes, the sweetest sentiments have the most sweeping appeal, swaying the hearts of even those unallied with the singer's causes. When he crooned "From the very first time I blessed my eyes on you, girl / My heart says, 'Follow through' " on "Waiting in Vain," one relives that

It was a time of paranoiac turmoil for Marley, who feared further attempts on his life, but also one of great artistic output.

love-at-first-sight rush, and it's nearly impossible to resist the tenderness. The innate groove and coaxing rhythm, so perfectly laid down by the Wailers, perfectly harmonized with their frontman's charismatic stage presence and inspired lyricism. If your hips don't start swaying or your toes begin tapping when "Jamming" comes blaring out of the speakers, there's something seriously wrong with you.

When U2's Bono posthumously inducted the dreadlocked mystic into the Rock and Roll Hall of Fame, the Irish frontman waxed poetic on the true substance of Marley's legend; "[Rock stars] love the extremes and [they're] expected to choose: the mud of the blues or the oxygen of the gospel, the hellhounds on our trail or the band of angels. Well, Bob Marley didn't choose or walk down the middle. He raced to the edges, embracing all extremes, creating a oneness. His oneness." To this day, and for many more days yet to come, Bob Marley remains a spiritualized hero, a figure of divine proportions whose music and message made him an icon around the world. N.M.

Born to Run

BRUCE SPRINGSTEEN

BORN TO RUN

COMPACT
DISC
DIGITAL AUDIO

COLUMBIA 1975

Bruce Springsteen:
guitar, vocals,
harmonica

Garry Tallent:
bass

Max M. Weinberg:
drums

Roy Bittan:
piano, organ,
harpsichord,
glockenspiel

**Clarence
Clemons:**
saxophone

Danny Federici:
organ

Steve Van Zandt:
background
vocals
("Thunder Road")

**Ernest "Boom"
Carter:**
drums
("Born to Run")

Richard Davis:
bass ("Meeting
Across the River")

David Sancious:
keyboards
("Born to Run")

Suki Lahav:
violin

**Randy Brecker,
Michael Brecker,
Dave Sanborn,
Wayne Andre:**
horns

Produced by
Bruce
Springsteen,
Jon Landau,
Mike Appel

Forget the music for a moment. *Born to Run* is one of the great short-story collections of the second half of the twentieth century. From the moment "the screen door slams," and "Mary's dress waves" in the opening line of "Thunder Road," through the setting of "one soft infested summer" on "Backstreets," to the album's finale, the "Jungleland" showdown " 'neath that giant Exxon sign that brings this fair city light," we are held mesmerized by a master storyteller.

A rock 'n' roll symphony as well, *Born to Run* is a glorious fusion of lyrics and energy, of imagery and passion. I was thirteen years old when it was released. I am from New Jersey, but I never worked in a factory or liked fast·cars, and my family only visited the shore maybe twice a summer. But like Faulkner, Steinbeck, Roth, and Cheever, the Boss made his specific stories of reluctant heroes universal—their desire to escape the mundane, their desperate attempts to carve out a little happiness, the struggle of ordinary people to lead extraordinary lives, their quest for romance both idealized ("she's so pretty that you're lost in the stars") and heart-wrenchingly realistic ("you ain't a beauty but hey, you're alright").

Bruce may be bitter about the "runaway American dream," but he understands the yearning. Everyone dreams on this album. In "Born to Run," Bruce laments how "this town rips the bones off your back," but that doesn't stop him from pledging to his girl that "I want to guard your dreams and visions." The working stiff longing for escape in "Night" is told that "you're just a prisoner of your dreams, holding on for your life." In the lush and poetic "Jungleland," the devastation comes not from a person or weapon, but in the end, "The Rat's own dream guns him down." And when the unnamed protagonist in "Meeting Across the River" tells Eddie that "tonight's gonna be everything that I said," we can feel the hope soaring in our chests, even as we know it will never work, that our hero and Eddie are always going to be wading in life's losing end.

"Born to Run" may be the greatest single in rock history. It is a heady rush, an adrenaline-packed, "fuel-injected" thrill ride—while the carefully crafted lyrics still linger hauntingly decades later. There is no slow build here. The anthem starts with a fury ("sprung from cages") and never subsides. Even when the Boss grunts his countdown into the final verse, we are with him. In a packed stadium or alone in our bedrooms, we are shrieking at the top of our lungs, our faces aglow from the bright sheen of exhilaration, the strings on our air guitars bursting from the onslaught of reclaimed bliss. If rock is release and freedom, there is no cut purer than this.

In his induction speech for Bruce at the Rock and Roll Hall of Fame, U2's Bono noted some of the differences between Springsteen and most rock stars. "No drug busts, no blood changes in Switzerland . . . No bad hair period, even in the eighties." This is because, for Bruce it was never about the fame, the girls, the drugs, the fast times. Bruce cared about one thing: the music. On *Born to Run,* we see the total focus on his art, the blood-letting sacrifice, the single-minded dedication that raises the merely great into the realm of the legendary and unforgettable.

At the close of "Jungleland," Springsteen quietly notes that "the poets down here don't write nothing at all, they just stand back and let it all be." Not in your case, Bruce. And definitely not on this album. H.C.

Patti Smith Horses

Horses

When *Horses* was released in the autumn of 1975, it attracted attention from several prominent critics as a portent of a new American "underground"—one that within a few months would become branded "punk." But to the uninitiated (i.e., those who never listened to the album), Patti Smith merely seemed to be another eccentric female singer/songwriter. There was little telling that within the next few years, the whole realm of women in rock was to transform mightily into a new kind of postfeminist angst that would have sweeping social and musical implications for the next three decades. Make no mistake about it— *Horses* heralded these changes, and Patti Smith was the harbinger of all that followed as far as genuine female liberation goes. Sure, artists like Grace Slick, Laura Nyro, Carole King, and Joni Mitchell had already explored sophisticated lyrical terrain as far as women's issues went, but Patti Smith, as an artist as well as a performer, was the first to convey the same confident sexuality as male per-

> **ARISTA RECORDS**
> 1975
> **Patti Smith:**
> vocals
> **Lenny Kaye:**
> guitars
> **Ivan Kral:**
> guitar, bass
> **Jay Dee Dougherty:**
> drums
> **Richard Sohl:**
> piano
> **Produced by**
> John Cale

formers but in a way that was still distinctly female. In order to understand the subsequent women-in-rock movement, it's important to realize that before Patti Smith came along, there was simply no one like Patti Smith. Sure, there had been aggressive female rock performers before, like Fanny or Suzi Quatro or to some extent even Janis Joplin. But Patti Smith not only defied the traditional role of women-in-rock, she provided an alternative that opened up a whole new universe of psychosexual implications—or what she called "the sea of possibility." And once the lid was off Pandora's box, there was no going back.

A perfect example of this transcendent quality was the opening track, her cover of Van Morrison's "Gloria." Few cover versions have ever so totally transformed a song into such a host of alternate visions. Not only did Smith and her band turn one of the most well-trodden riffs in rock into a whole new and stirring dynamic (partly as a result of pianist Richard Sohl's achingly baroque style), but the androgynous implications—the fact that Smith maintained the song's macho swagger and didn't change the gender of the lyrics—gave it a whole new, multifaceted meaning. As it stands, "Gloria," the first song most people heard by Patti Smith, is one of the greatest cover versions of any song ever.

She provided an alternative that opened up a whole new universe of psychosexual implications—or what she called "the sea of possibility." And once the lid was off Pandora's box, there was no going back.

All of the other songs on *Horses* were originals, fitting given that Smith had earned an underground reputation as a poet, another element she helped bring to rock (along with her friends Tom Verlaine and Richard Hell). In a way they were only doing what Bob Dylan had been doing—using words to challenge their listeners' conceptions about what one could and couldn't do within the framework of conventional song structure. Songs like "Birdland" and "Land," both more than nine minutes in length, were often described by critics as "phantasmagoric" due to the beatnik implications of the lyrics and the band's almost free-jazz approach to the music. Produced by Velvet Underground veteran John Cale, *Horses* firmly put Smith in the tradition of the New York underground, but her range was far wider, evoking everything from the smoky ambiance of Billie Holiday to the free-ranging expressiveness of the Beats. For a woman to draw these connections in 1975, and to encapsulate it all in a package that rocked effectively, was truly stunning. Patti Smith was in many ways a One-Woman Rock Preservation Society, and she saw herself in a boho-literary tradition that stretched all the way back to Rimbaud and Baudelaire and encompassed the Rolling Stones, Bob Marley, and Bob Dylan.

The band meanwhile was one of the most visionary of the time, combining the raw, energetic street feel of the Velvet Underground with jazz and film music ideas that made full-fledged freak-outs like "Birdland" among the most shocking rock performances of the era and placed the Patti Smith Group firmly in punk's top echelon before either the Ramones or the Sex Pistols came along. Along with Television, and Richard Hell's Voidoids, they were in many ways the first of the arty-punk practitioners, but in the case of the Patti Smith Group, they came about these conclusions on their own, since guitarist Lenny Kaye had begun accompanying Smith at poetry readings as far back as 1972.

Signed to Clive Davis's Arista records in 1975, Smith arrived right at the crossroads, smack dab in the middle of the cultural malaise known as the seventies. If any album made the future happen faster, it was *Horses*. Two and a half decades later, Smith is still reaping the rewards for her vision, and so are we. J.S.H.

Blood on the Tracks

For a sustained and regrettable period in my twenties, I spent a good portion of my time and energy in pursuit of a "Dylan girl." For this I blame *Blood on the Tracks*. Still, if I had to do it all again, I wouldn't spare myself the trouble if it meant never getting to hear the album.

Just what, exactly, a "Dylan girl" *was* is hard to say, but I think the general idea was a tall, shapely woman who managed to exemplify the essentially bittersweet character of love.

Blood on the Tracks might seem an odd inspiration for romantic reverie. Among Dylan fans,

it has a reputation as "the divorce album." (It was, in fact, written and recorded while Dylan was still married to first wife Sara Lowndes—which may mean that cause and effect have been reckoned exactly backward.) It is a work that is steeped in raw-throated, searing loss. Love is everywhere in these songs but seldom in the present. It drifts on the currents of the past, to wash inexorably on the shores of the present. Some of Dylan's "I"s (for this is a collection of songs told almost entirely in the first person) are resigned to love's passing and some rail at it in a spitting fury, but all are haunted by it.

Dylan is hardly the first to sing about broken hearts. He succeeds so completely here not because his characters are unlucky in love but because he manages to convey just how much they have lost. Working backward from all the pain, you can catch teasing glimpses of relationships of great and fragile beauty. And, having sent love soaring on gossamer wings, Dylan has few songwriting peers when it comes to documenting the moment "when it all comes crashing down," as it does in "Tangled Up in Blue" and so many other places on this album.

It's not just his songwriting that does the job. The classic knock on Dylan is that he's got a terrible voice, grating at best. Even the most dedicated Dylan fan—and probably Dylan himself—would allow that there are times when this is true. On *Blood on the Tracks*, however, he reveals himself as one of the great interpretive singers in popular music. The examples are many: the long "ohhh" before he delivers the punch line in each verse of "You're a Big Girl

COLUMBIA
1974
Bob Dylan:
vocals, guitars, harmonica
Tony Brown:
bass
Buddy Cage:
steel guitar
Paul Griffin:
organ
Eric Weissberg & Deliverance
Produced by
Bob Dylan

Now," by turns thoughtful, stricken, knowing, defeated; the uncanny blend of bravado and grief with which he imbues the line "Say for me that I'm all right" in "If You See Her, Say Hello"; his channeling of, first, paranoia ("Someone's got it in for me . . .") and then indignant rage (". . . they're planting stories in the preeeeeeeheeeeus!") in the opening gusts of "Idiot Wind." The effect is of lovers who have lost control, but he achieves this through one of the most focused vocal performances ever recorded.

Blood on the Tracks can make you feel morbidly good about feeling bad. Not surprisingly, it is the perfect soundtrack to a breakup. Its particular brand of sadness primes the wounded heart for another giddy flight—and for another exquisite spiral earthward.

It's an album that transforms the soul's cruelest tortures into magnificent art, and that's the sort of thing that can set you out in search of "a Dylan girl," however bad an idea that is in practice.   E.W.

30

I Never Loved a Man the Way I Love You

I Never Loved a Man the Way I Love You, her first fully realized album, made Aretha Franklin the undisputed "Queen of Soul." The set was produced by label bigwig Jerry Wexler, who also penned the boastful liner notes extolling Aretha's qualities as a superstar. She didn't just have the qualities—Aretha epitomized superstardom, crossing over from the soul charts into the popular mainstream. An ardent singer who knew no boundaries, Aretha would be equally at home next to Janis Joplin or Etta James.

Opening with a fiery transformation of the Otis Redding classic "Respect," Aretha lets you know from the get-go that she would be taking no prisoners. "R-E-S-P-E-C-T / Find out what it means to me." And boy, does she let you know what it means to her. Women would flock to the song as a battle cry for feminism and liberation, while the men would be drawn to its irresistible dance-floor sensibility. The backing vox came courtesy of Aretha's true-life sisters Carolyn and Erma, who belt out their "sock-it-to-me's" with inspired abandon.

The album was recorded over the course of a month. The singer cowrote four of the eleven tracks, allowing her personality and emotionality to seep into the music for the first time. The others she assembled for recording included a smoky version of Sam Cooke's "A Change Is Gonna Come," the torch ballad "Do Right Woman—Do Right Man," and the slow-grooving title track. Love was the central theme for this project, and Aretha explored the whole spectrum.

There are few albums that can skate so easily from emotion to emotion without feeling contrived, but Aretha's sincerity, conviction, and reverence for her craft shines through on every track. *I Never Loved a Man...* stands as a reflection and an interpretation of our own lives, reminding us that heartache and passion are a part of the road we walk. With Aretha as guide, a broken heart never felt so good.

N.M.

ATLANTIC RECORDS
1967

Aretha Franklin:
piano, vocals

Tommy Cogbill:
bass

Dewey Oldham:
keyboards

Carolyn Franklin:
background vocals

Jimmy Johnson:
guitar

Chips Moman:
guitar

Melvin Lastie:
cornet, trumpet

**Willie Bridges,
King Curtis, Charles
Chalmers:**
saxophone

Produced by
Jerry Wexler

Innervisions

One of the all-time great one-man band albums: While Stevie Wonder wasn't entirely devoid of outside instrumental support on this opus, he played an inordinate amount of instrumental tracks himself, paving the way for Prince and other studio-reclusive tortured-geniuses later on.

Innervisions also represents Wonder's full embrace of the ARP synthesizer, a common motif among musicians at the time because of its ability to construct a complete sound environment. What could be better for a one-man band? Where white artists like Pete Townshend, Paul McCartney, and Todd Rundgren had already introduced the instrument to rock audiences, Stevie Wonder was the first black artist to experiment with this technology on a mass scale, and *Innervisions* was hugely influential on the subsequent future of commercial black music. Wonder had first fooled around with the instrument on his prior, also excellent LP, *Talking Book*. By the time of *Innervisions*, the rubbery funk of "Superstition" had given way to even more elasticized rhythms of the apocalyptic "Higher Ground."

Speaking of apocalypse, *Innervisions'* opening cut, "Too High," states plainly what Stevie's intentions are on this LP: mainly, acute social commentary on the state of the black community. As he urges a brother to come down from the clouds, Wonder's voice scales to new falsetto heights, showing his innovativeness as a vocalist as well as a social commentator. "Golden Lady," meanwhile, looks askance at a materialistic sister who's willing to compromise her spiritual integrity for monetary gifts. The whole message of this album seems to be caution—Wonder seems to be warning the black community to be aware of their own plight, strive for improvement, and take matters into their own hands. But this is all against the backdrop of the harsh social realities of America circa 1973, and nowhere does this conflict hit home more than in Wonder's magnum opus, "Living for the City," a raw piece of modern blues on which Wonder played every instrument. The message of urban struggle resonates even more strongly now than it did thirty years ago, proving that the "inner-visions" of this LP were visionary as well. J.S.H.

TAMLA
1973
Stevie Wonder:
vocals, piano, synthesizer, bass, drums, guitar
Various musicians
Produced by
Robert Margouleff

Moondance

By the time *Moondance* came out, Van Morrison was absolutely untouchable in the minds of critics. Coming off the cult classic *Astral Weeks,* which was unanimously rejoiced over upon its release in 1968, Morrison was a mystic visionary who'd yet to find his niche with the public even as the critics sang his praises. *Moondance* was the album that finally solved this impasse: While *Astral Weeks* had been an obscure song cycle with troubling themes, *Moondance* was effervescent and self-affirming. Part of the reason was that Morrison had recently settled into a life of domestic bliss. What it was all part of was the rock aging process, which began in earnest at just about the same time as the sixties turned into the seventies. Morrison, who'd been a teen idol in his native Ireland with his hardcore R&B band, Them, was now coming to terms with himself as an artist, and *Moondance* was an enormous step in his progress.

It was also the album that established Morrison as an FM radio staple in the early seventies, with songs like "Moondance," "Caravan," and "Into the Mystic." The album represented a new kind of songwriting for the artist— whereas *Astral Weeks* had been brooding and poetic, (a mode Morrison would return to later on with idiosyncratic albums like *Saint Dominic's Preview*, *Veedon Fleece* and *Into the Music*), *Moondance* was rustic and earthy, the songs based on more conventionally melodic musical figures. This was partly due to Morrison's new band, whose even-tempered intuition helped keep Morrison focused. As a result, songs like "And It Stoned Me" and "Crazy Love" revealed an artist almost giddy with natural wonder. Not surprisingly, the album was a big hit among hippie couples settling into complacent domesticity—once again, along with the work of Crosby, Stills, Nash & Young, James Taylor, and Paul McCartney, it was a harbinger of "adult rock" being born.

"Moondance" was an evocative number set to a waltz tempo with jazzy undertones provided by piano and saxophone—the romantic splendor of the lyrics, and Morrison's phrasing, was scintillating in its sexual jubilation. There aren't many songs, then or now, that sound like this, and it's easy to see why it is ranked among Morrison's most stellar performances. Another lyrical obsession on this album was the mystifying powers of the music itself. "Into the Mystic," for instance, utilizes a rolling, soulful texture to explore the intricate balance between life's natural wonder and the cosmic harmony of the universe. As he quips at the end of the song, "it's too late to stop now." In "Caravan," one of his greatest songs, he celebrates the transcendent powers of rock 'n' roll and the spontaneous pleasure of listening to a great radio station and not knowing what song is going to come on next. Morrison, who'd continue to make interesting music for the remainder of the decade, navigated his own course with equal spontaneity.   J.S.H.

WARNER BROS.
1970

Van Morrison:
vocals

Jeff Labes:
keyboards, percussion, clavinet

Gary Malaber:
drums

David Shaw:
percussion

Colin Tilton:
flute, tenor sax

John Klingberg:
bass

Guy Masson:
conga

John Platania:
guitar

Jack Shroener:
tenor and soprano sax

Cissy Houston, Emily Houston, Judy Clay, Jackie Verdell:
backing vocals

Produced by
Van Morrison

Sex Machine

I DJ once and a while in bars and stuff and when things are kind of quiet or kind of slow I put on some James Brown and the dance floor fills right up and everybody starts hoppin', hootin' and hollerin.'   —BUN E. CARLOS, CHEAP TRICK

When James Brown recorded this album he was inarguably one of the pivotal figures in black music at a time when black music—and black culture—was becoming more tumultuous by the moment. Turbulent polyrhythms meant to mirror the troubled times were being worked into the firmament of R&B via a whole new school of black musicians plying a riff-heavy brand of expression that would soon become known as Funk. There was Sly Stone, with his fully integrated rock-soul-funk merger; there was Miles Davis, with the back-to-Africa boogaloo of *Bitches Brew;* and there was James Brown, whose populist message—"Say It Loud—I'm Black and I'm Proud"—rang true throughout the black community. For Brown to come along and dump this two-record live set in the midst of all that, sermonizing sex as salvation, was akin to a minister hailing his congregation. The politics of the future would be increasingly physical.

    The subsequent history of black popular music, from disco to hip-hop, can be laid at the feet of "Sex Machine," with its horizontal cadence, scratchy guitars, and orgasmic bridge where a piano dances across the bar with dynamic call-and-response rhythms. It was on this song that Brown's whole accent-on-the-one rhythmic concept—which he'd been working on since 1964—finally took over completely. The result was a more rubbery type of funk rhythm that loaned itself excellently to lascivious excess. In a few years, there'd be whole disco suites based on such rhythms to supposedly serenade the strains of bed-jamming. "I feel like getting into it / *DOIN'* it, y' know?" James Brown yells during the intro, and "Sex Machine" was a healthy blast of sexual proselytizing before Al Green and Marvin Gaye made such things commonplace.

Sex Machine was also the first James Brown album to feature a hot new young bass player named Bootsy Collins, who was only seventeen at the time this album was recorded. Songs like "Give It Up or Turn It Loose" and "Licking Stick Licking Stick" were prime examples of the new slap-bass style that would come to character-

KING
1970
James Brown:
vocals, organ
Bobby Byrd:
vocals, organ
Clyde Stubblefield:
drums
Fred Wesley:
trombone
Bootsy Collins:
bass
Jimmy Nolen:
guitars
Maceo Parker:
tenor saxophone
Richard Griffith:
trumpet
Joseph Davis:
trumpet
Marva Whitney:
background vocals
Produced by
James Brown

ize funk. It was a short-lived collaboration, however, seeing as Collins soon left James Brown (on less-than-amiable terms) to join the funk mothership, Parliament-Funkadelic. In the meantime, all subsequent incarnations of the artist would exert a more profound funk groove. It all began with this album, which was really James Brown's first attempt to pull off a sustained jam for several minutes, leading to excursions like *Revolution of the Mind* and *The Payback*, which were heavy on the extended funk outings.

Although this album was supposedly recorded live in James Brown's hometown of Augusta, Georgia, there was some debate at the time whether it was indeed "live," since there's a chance that some of the live applause was dubbed ("I Got the Feelin' " sounds exactly like the single version). Still, only a ham like James Brown would play Blood, Sweat and Tears' "Spinning Wheel" as an overwrought organ-laden fest with this much aplomb—audience or no. J.S.H.

35 Sign "O" the Times

That Prince sure is an unusual fellow. He's a first-rate singer/songwriter. He's a commanding force on any instrument he cares to pick up. He's responsible for some of the loopiest lyrics ever penned. And when it comes to his principal interests—sex and God—he ventures beyond mere obsession into flat-out weirdness. On *Sign "O" the Times*, Prince played all these extraordinary qualities to the hilt and came up with a double album that's a modern rock 'n' soul classic.

Although the album kicks off with the stark, despondent title track (a rare foray into social commentary referring to AIDS, drug addiction, and the *Challenger* space shuttle explosion), its mood soon lifts. "It" and "Hot Thing" are Prince at his most lascivious, while the touching "Forever in My Life" and the unusually humble "I Could Never Take the Place of Your Man" stress the importance of long-term romantic commitment. "The Cross," a weighty rock anthem, finds Prince looking to heaven for guidance, and the closing "Adore" merges the spiritual and the carnal in a falsetto vocal tour de force.

Of course, *Sign "O" the Times* wouldn't be a proper Prince album without a touch of the bizarre. Four of its songs feature a mysterious lead vocalist named Camille, who sounds suspiciously like Prince sped up a few notches. Camille's big number is "If I Was Your Girlfriend," a baffling piece of psychodrama including the line "Would you run to me if somebody hurt you / Even if that somebody was me?"

Divesting himself of his band, the Revolution (they appear on only one song, "It's Gonna Be a Beautiful Night," the tightest slice of funk you'll hear this side of James Brown), the Purple One returned to his wunderkind ways. With a few exceptions, most notably guest spots by protégés Sheila E. and Sheena Easton on "U Got the Look," Prince plays and sings everything here. As the stop-on-a-dime intricacies of "Play in the Sunshine" and the pounding pulse of "Strange Relationship" demonstrate, he's his own best accompanist.   M.R.

PAISLEY PARK / WARNER BROS.
1987

Prince:
vocals, guitars, keyboards, bass, drums, percussion

Eric Leeds:
saxophone

Atlanta Bliss:
trumpet

Various guest musicians

Produced by
Prince

Off the Wall

Before plastic surgery, oxygen tanks, Neverland, and constant scandal, Michael Jackson began his solo musical legacy with the glitterific and Quincy Jonesified *Off the Wall*. This album personified everything that was behind the velvet ropes at Studio 54, reflected off the disco balls and rolling under the wheels of skaters in rinks across the U.S. and beyond. Michael captured a time that was bridged between an era of glamour and the beginning of the "Me Decade" by claiming "So, tonight, gotta leave that nine-to-five upon the shelf, and just enjoy yourself."

Kicking off the album is the infectious groove of "Don't Stop 'Til You Get Enough." With its bass-and-cowbell aphrodisiac, the song is still a driving force on the dance floor almost a quarter of a century later. A perfect guarantee and DJ staple of booty-shakin', hip-gyrating, get-the-crowd-jumping anthem for all colors, races, and sexual orientations. "Rock with You" was the "time-to-apply-the-Bonnebell-lipgloss" couples-only skating classic. Plush with violins and a slow groove, any guy had a chance with this flirtatious embrace. Obviously, lovers across the dance floors felt the same, since it sashayed to number one on the charts for four weeks. The title track was another party anthem

that begged the listener to drop everything and grab a dance partner. "Working Day and Night," "She's Out of My Life," "Girlfriend," and others complete this masterpiece that seeped disco into the hearts of disbelievers of all musical genres.

The gatefold cover of featured a now refreshing, untouched Michael Jackson in his purest state, almost the complete opposite of the barely recognizable Michael of today. His body language is open, the hair is natural, and his trademark white socks and black loafers make their debut. His almost innocent and naive grin is reminiscent of a college freshman, full of hope and an uncompromising quest for individuality. Michael graduated from his band of brothers and began to "ease on down the road" to the self-proclaimed title "King of Pop." I invite Michael to stop his yearning to find his youth through surgery, amusement rides, and space journeys and take an afternoon to really soak in the one-of-a-kind brilliance that his young self created. He just might find the youth serum he's been looking for. R.B.

EPIC/CBS RECORDS
1979
Michael Jackson:
vocals
Various musicians

Produced by
Quincy Jones
Coproduced by
Michael Jackson

The Miseducation of Lauryn Hill

When the Fugees's sophomore album *The Score* vaulted the group to multi-platinum success, the world became infatuated with sweet faced and golden throated frontwoman Lauryn Hill. Hill was the fabulous component of the ghetto fabulous image that she, producer/rapper Wyclef Jean, and rapper Praz projected. And for every slick lick and hip pop hook Wyclef Jean created for the New Jersey trio, Hill provided the soulful vocalizing and spiritualized lyricism. It was the perfect combination of the commercially palatable and the critically lovable. However, when it was announced that the Fugees were going to 'take a break,' while all the members pursued solo projects, pundits weren't so sure that any of the parts would rival the greatness of the whole. So, when *The Miseducation of Lauryn Hill* dropped, people were astonished at and in awe of the impressive solo salvo.

The Miseducation of Lauryn Hill serves as the opinionated MC's declaration of independence and intent. The scathing opening number "Lost Ones" seemed to be an indictment of her time with the Fugees and her long-rumored affair with Jean, as she spit sweet venom with lines like "Never underestimate those who you scar / 'Cause karma, karma, karma comes back to you hard." Then on "Superstar," she vindictively rhymes "Just as Christ was a superstar, you stupid star / They'll hail you then they'll nail you, no matter who you are." Yet, despite all the allusions to her past conflicts, the true theme of the album is one of questing—be that for love, artistic fulfillment, spiritual enlightenment, or personal well-being. "Let's love ourselves then we can't fail / to make a better situation."

Musically, it was a deftly blended mixture of hip-hop beats, reggae guitar riffing, soul licks, and R&B croons. Impressively, Hill had fashioned an album that was as accessible to her urban fan base, as it was to mall hopping teens and a baby boomer crowd fueled by critically acclaimed curiosity. Even the guys had to admit that it wasn't a Lilith-inspired series of rants, rather just a different perspective on the very same world they played in, and therefore very worhty to be pumped on their own stereos. In fact, the first single, "Doo Wop (That Thing),"

> **RUFFHOUSE/ COLUMBIA RECORDS**
> 1998
> **Lauryn Hill**
> vocals
> **Various Musicians**
> **Produced by**
> Lauryn Hill

was Hill's own bittersweet warning to the girls and the guys to watch out for those with less than good intentions. Though others preached to hate the game, not the player, Hill was more than ready to call out the players on both sides of the fence and implicate them for their crimes of the heart. "'Member when he told you he was 'bout the Benjamins / You act like you ain't hear him then gave him a little trim."

The Miseducation of Lauryn Hill would spawn a trio of MTV and radio hits, "Ex-Factor," "Everything Is Everything," and "Doo Wop (That Thing)," and rack up sales surpassing 8 million copies in the U.S. alone. She took home five golden gramophones at the Grammies that year, including the prestigious "Album of the Year" trophy, and had no problem snagging a few moonmen from MTV at the Video Music Awards. Even long after those awards have gathered dust on a mantelpiece somewhere, *The Miseducation of Lauryn Hill* will still stand as a truly inspired album with a timeless sensibility.   N . M .

38

Hotel California

These cosmic cowboys are the most she-bedazzlin' bunch o' macho lady-killers to ever kick up dust on the dirt trail and *Hotel California* represents the epitome of mid-seventies "laidback" *laissez faire* El Lay easy livin'. From the fandango-like opening strains of the title cut to he wistful dying gasps of "The Last Resort" (get the obvious pun) this is amongst the pre-eminent "concept" albums of the seventies. By 1976, the Eagles found themselves trapped on the treadmill of the corporate rock gravy train and they responded with a cynical look at the trappings of their success and the sometime superficial netherworld of life in the business of fast—and ultimately hollow—dreams. Although the Eagles have oft been criticized for being *victims* of this very soul-destroying process, *Hotel California* is actually a somewhat ironic *commentary* on the whole Hollywood myth-making process, as reflected by the anthem, "Life in the Fast Lane," often mistaken as pure burn-out rock by the party hordes of the late seventies, but actu-

ASYLUM
1976

Don Henley:
vocals, drums
Glenn Frey:
vocals, guitar, piano
Randy Meisner:
bass, vocals
Joe Walsh:
guitar
Don Felder:
guitar, vocals

Produced by
Bill Szymczyk

ally a cynical look at all that was superficial about the era (particularly in Los Angeles where the Eagles called home). It was a theme they would explore at even greater lengths in songs like "King of L.A." on *The Long Run*. Far from being sympathetic to the decadence that surrounded them, the Eagles were actually taking a squinty-eyed stance on this album. *Hotel California* also marks the emergence of Don Henley as the band's chief songwriter. Take, for example, the lilting "New Kid in the Town," which tells the tale of a stud pulling up his stirrups in the protagonist's own corral—much to his chagrin of course. "I don't want to hear it," Henley laments as he watches his own cowgirl go prancing off into the sunset on the arms of this able-bodied cocksman. It was the L.A. of Warren Beatty and Jerry Brown, and it was a world the Eagles knew well. *Hotel California* epitomizes that world, and for this reason, it's a perfect snapshot of the fondue cocaine culture and the best L.A. album of all time.   A . D . S .

Tapestry

Carole King's *Tapestry* is one of the best-selling albums of all time, with a handful of songs ubiquitous to anyone with even the most passing interest in popular music. Consequently, it is easy to forget the fact that there were just about no expectations for the album when it was released.

King first came to fame as half of one of the most successful songwriting teams of the sixties, with her then-husband, Gerry Goffin. Together, they wrote some of the most enduring songs in pop music, including "The Loco-motion," "Up On the Roof," "Don't Bring Me Down," and "Chains," the latter of which was covered by the Beatles (Lennon and McCartney cited Goffin/King as a major influence). In 1968, Goffin and King divorced, and King went on to form her own short-lived band, the City, which featured guitarist Danny Kortchmar. Through Kortchmar, King soon became friends with up-and-coming singer-songwriter, James Taylor, who encouraged her to kick off her solo career. Her 1970 solo debut, *Writer*, was a commercial flop, leading many to believe that

EPIC RECORDS
1971
Carole King:
vocals, keyboards
James Taylor:
acoustic guitar
Danny Kortchmar:
guitar, conga
Russ Kunkel:
drums
Joel O'Brien:
drums
Charles Larkey:
bass, string bass
Additional Musicians
Produced by
Lou Adler

her lot in life was writing for others, not performing her own music. Of course, anyone too vocally of that opinion would soon be eating serious crow.

Her second album, *Tapestry*, struck a chord with the public in a big way, remaining on the charts for over five years. King turned out to be exactly the type of artist that would be hugely successful in the seventies: a singer-songwriter, preferring confessional, personal songs to protest anthems, and eschewing sixties psychedelia for strong songwriting and clear recording values. On the other hand, while her debut as a solo artist was (unintentionally) well timed, *Tapestry* itself is timeless. Some of the songs were tried and true: "Will You Still Love Me Tomorrow?" and "(You Make Me Feel Like) A Natural Woman" were both hits she and Goffin had penned for other artists. There were also several new songs which would be just as successful, including "I Feel The Earth Move," "So Far Away," and "It's Too Late." Decades later, the album plays like a seamless body of work. B.I.

Astral Weeks

It might be the best record of original thought that anybody's ever made. It's so completely unlike anything that went before it. You can sort of hear the influence of certain kinds of music upon it, but . . . it seems to flow completely free of it. And the vocal performances are the freest that I think Van ever recorded. I suppose it's a one of a kind thing—he could have never repeated it.   —ELVIS COSTELLO

I first heard *Astral Weeks* in the winter of 1990. Oh, I'd owned it for some years before that, and had listened to it occasionally, but the first time I *heard* it I was alone, in San Francisco, in an apartment 'til then occupied by two people, now suddenly occupied by one. Until that time, I suppose, I'd reckoned the album was "jazz," not a compliment in my Ramones-fed lexicon of thug rock, art punk, and garage junk. I liked the Stooges, Sonic Youth, cranky guitars of every stripe. (This was perhaps one reason why my apartment's tenancy was suddenly halved. But I

digress.) Here was an album that led with the bass. That had flutes on it. But hearing it, then, suddenly—the nimble surge of Richard Davis's bass that kicks off the title track, Van's soul-sick, questing vocal itself almost an instrument, almost scat, though nothing so corny—I understood. It *was* jazz—indeed, Davis had played in Eric Dolphy's band—but in a good way. These songs were not verse-chorus-verse (or simply verse-chorus-chorus-chorus, the way I really liked 'em), they were meditations. Extremely beautiful meditations: that bass was the anchor, the buoyant pulse-beat around which the whole album spun, acoustic guitar used mostly as a rhythm instrument, or for coloring. There were, indeed, flutes. And exquisite violins, as in the devastating "Cypress Avenue," where for a moment the song, and perhaps the listener—I did, anyway—shakes like a tree in a windstorm. Atop it all, there is Van. Who proves, on this album first, he is a poet.

For this is miles away from the clap-happy pop of "Brown-Eyed Girl" and the shout-along, short-witted pleasures of "Gloria." This record is a document—though of what, precisely, it is difficult to decipher. Love, surely, as the swirling, rhapsodic "Sweet Thing" and the flamenco-ish "The Way That Young Lovers Do" make clear. Loss of love, also, as the stark, cryptic "Slim Slow Slider"—the last of the album's eight songs (though "songs" here seems too reductive a term)—makes it a little less clear. The record's intense, near-impenetrable privacy

---

WARNER BROS.
1968

Van Morrison:
guitar, keyboards, sax, vocals

Jay Berliner:
guitar

Richard Davis:
bass

Connie Kay:
drums

John Payne:
flute, sax

Warren Smith:
percussion, vibraphone

Produced by
Lewis Menenstein

(rumor has it Morrison recorded his vocals in a studio closet and refused to speak to the band) only furthers the mystery. What is going on at the party described in, and thrown by the transvestite, "Madame George?" Is "Cypress Avenue" really, as it appears to be, about a pederast watching schoolchildren pass? Morrison's phrasing—his stuttering repetitions and Belfast accent—make it tough to tell. And those gorgeous, elastic vocals of his ensure that it doesn't matter one bit, if the literal and the imagined meanings of these songs don't quite align. Indeed that may be exactly what the album's about. But it's no wonder, really, that this record confounded me as a callow twenty-one-year old; nor that it was suddenly comprehensible to me as a heartbroken adult. Years later, when his fire had somewhat dimmed, Morrison would be reduced to titling an album *Inarticulate Speech of the Heart*. Here, as an obviously less callow twenty-one-year-old, he gave extraordinary shape to exactly that.   M.S.

Lady Soul

If you had to sum up her music in one word, the choice would be simple: Power.... Aretha used that power to establish herself once and for all as a leading figure in popular music.

Scholarly dissertations could be written about the emotional resonance of Aretha Franklin's singing, about the layers of meaning in every one of her "ow"s and "hoo"s, about the uncanny way in which she blends assertiveness and vulnerability. But if you had to sum up her music in one word, the choice would be simple: Power. In 1967, with the album *I Never Loved a Man the Way I Love You* and its epochal remake of Otis Redding's "Respect," Aretha used that power to establish herself once and for all as a leading figure in popular music. On her 1968 followup, she upped the ante, staking her claim to the imposing title of *Lady Soul.*

From the first swampy, baritone guitar-propelled seconds of "Chain of Fools," Franklin proved that the title was well deserved. There's no noodling around here, none of the labored vocal gymnastics that bog down so much modern R&B. Aretha aims straight for the heart, hitting her target every time. Listen to the gospel-like heights her voice achieves in the album's centerpiece, the classic "(You Make Me Feel Like) A Natural Woman," written for her by sixties hitmakers Carole King and Gerry Goffin. Despite her obvious mastery of technique, her singing never sounds practiced or planned; it has all the spontaneity of a tidal wave or a volcanic eruption. That said, she knows to save her best stuff for the end of a song. Check out how she repeatedly milks the

words "You just thank the Lord" at the climax of her sublime cover of Curtis Mayfield's "People Get Ready," or the wild whoops and hollers she unleashes in the waning moments of "Good to Me as I Am to You"—they make guest Eric Clapton's biting guitar fills seem cluttered by comparison.

Aretha's ability to be intense and casual at the same time was perfectly matched by her backing musicians. Listen to the groove they cook up for "Niki Hoeky," relentless in its drive yet somehow nonchalant. Hear the tenderness they bring to "(You Make Me Feel Like) A Natural Woman," mirroring the earthy spirituality in Franklin's voice. Such playing made the words "Muscle Shoals"— the name of the Alabama town where Aretha recorded—a synonym for classic soul. And if you don't know what that is, you need this album.

M.R.

ATLANTIC
1968
Aretha Franklin:
vocals, piano
Carolyn Franklin:
vocals
The Sweet Inspirations:
backing vocals
Spooner Oldham:
electric piano, organ
**Jimmy Johnson,
Bobby Womack,
Joe South:**
guitars
**Mel Lastie,
Joe Newman,
Bernie Glow:**
trumpets
King Curtis:
tenor sax
**Selden Powell,
Frank Wess:**
tenor sax, flute
Haywood Henry:
baritone sax
Tony Studd:
bass trombone
Warren Smith:
vibraharp
Tom Cogbill:
bass
Roger Hawkins:
drums
Produced by
Jerry Wexler

Appetite for Destruction

GEFFEN
1987
Axl Rose:
vocals
Slash, Izzy Stradlin:
guitars
Duff "Rose" McKagen:
bass
Steven Adler:
drums
Produced by
Mike Clink

In the annals of rock 'n' roll, every few years, as the music reaches extended periods of complacency, an artist comes along to spearhead what usually gets branded as a "rock revival" (we see this happening right now in the form of the Strokes and their ilk). As an era, the mid-eighties were just about the epitome of stake-in-the-heart lying-down-and-dying inactivity for real rock 'n' roll. Being the era of high-tech innovations, the very sound of what was then being passed off as "rock 'n' roll" had come to mean whizzing synths and crackling snapdrums. Guitars were nary heard in the mix, nor were thundering hard-rock rhythm sections or screeching vocals. The whole "just say no" dictum of the Reagan era had in many ways gutted the "bad-boy" quotient that had always been so much a part of rock, and most of the so-called "rock stars" of the day seemed more poised for matinee-idol status than rabble-rousing effrontery.

Then came Guns N' Roses: with an arrogant, leonine-maned lead singer who undulated around the microphone in the tradition of such other classic serpentine frontmen as Mick Jagger and Steven Tyler, and a thuggish bunch of stylishly-coiffed so-ugly-they-were-beautiful backup men, including the reptilian guitarist Slash, who played the perfect Keith Richards counterpart to Axl Rose's Mick Jagger. Guns N' Roses were like a throwback to the decadent and somewhat dangerous ethos of the mid-seventies when bands with excessive habits like Led Zeppelin and Aerosmith stormed into town like invading warriors wreaking havoc.

Earning its chops on the L.A. club scene in the early eighties, Guns N' Roses didn't fall victim to the vapid kissy-poo of their peers like Poison or Cinderella. *Appetite for Destruction* was, as its title suggests, a molten blast of street rock 'n' roll from start to finish: "Night Train" was a party anthem to rival AC/DC, a mad celebration of the sauce that had Axl lamenting "I crash and burn/I never learn." such sentiment also adorned the self-destructive opus, "Mr. Brownstone," which graphically detailed the band's clandestine drug escapades on the wrong side of town to the tune of a crashing riff. Similarly, the anthem "Welcome to the Jungle" was about all the young sheep straight off the bus from places like Indiana who were lured into the Hollywood nighttime world—kids not unlike the young Axl Rose, which is why the song's message resonated instead of coming

off like an empty boast. But it wasn't all doom and gloom with the Guns N' Roses boys: "Paradise City" was stomping party anthem in the seventies tradition that shook out the cobwebs of Reaganism at a time when we needed it most.

Slash proved himself capable of the same kind of fret-flaying mastery on his axe as such previous guitar gods as Jimmy Page, Ted Nugent, and Angus Young, while Axl was an original vocalist who alternated between a boozer-redneck drawl and a more typically "heavy metal" yelp (as epitomized by the band's first big hit and the album opener, "Welcome to the Jungle"). "Sweet Child o' Mine," the album's biggest hit, redefined the "power ballad" in the day and age when rock video production was reaching its zenith and made Guns N' Roses a household name.

The band proved unable to handle such stardom and their recordings faltered, but *Appetite* still stands as one of the definitive fist-pumping hard-rock opuses, able to ignite any flashpot-happy horde of rabid rock fans to this day. In many ways, Guns N' Roses can even be seen as the catalysts for the move back toward guitar-oriented rock which peaked with Nirvana, another band signed to Geffen a few years later.　　　J.S.H.

Led Zeppelin II

ATLANTIC
1969
Jimmy Page:
guitar
Robert Plant:
vocals, harmonica
John Paul Jones:
bass, keyboards
John Bonham:
drums
Produced by
Jimmy Page

When Led Zeppelin waxed *Led Zeppelin II*, they were still in the process of proving themselves to the American critics and public. The going had been rough for the young Brits, but slowly they were gaining their wings, establishing a reputation as an electrifying live attraction that carried out its assault with ruthless aplomb. Already their tours were legend as they made their way across America for the first time like Vikings storming into the nearest village to pillage everyone and everything that stood in their path. *Led*

Zeppelin II was, in many ways, the triumphant vindication of these excesses, and it established a precedent for the band that they'd continue to build on halfway through the next decade as they established themselves as perhaps the preeminent rock royalty, and the prototype heavy metal band, making the way for everyone from Queen to Aerosmith to AC/DC.

The band's first album, *Led Zeppelin*, released earlier in 1969, was still a continuation of Page's work in the Yardbirds—at least a couple of the songs still dated from that period, and the approach was still bluesy (albeit much more intense). By the time of *Zep II*, the blues was still very much a part of Zeppelin's overall sound, as it would always be, but now the blues had become supersonic—the opening chords of "Whole Lotta Love" told the story: Singer Robert Plant coughs, an arrogant gesture in itself, as Page begins hammering out a staccato guitar riff that would serve as one of the all-time metal prototypes (right up there with Deep Purple's "Smoke on the Water" and Aerosmith's "Walk This Way"). Meanwhile, the sentiment was menacing—the swaggering guitars and Plant's white-cat-in-heat howl underscored the brutal sexuality that lurked underneath what was essentially an old blues number. John Bonham's thundering percussion, miked so it sounded as if he was sitting right in the middle of the ensemble (thus adding "gravity"), only reinforced the macho swagger. This was a whole new kind of rock—it wasn't about seduction, it was about dominance. Above all, it was about brute force.

The great rock critic Lester Bangs once suggested that the root of heavy metal was musicians trying to come to terms with all the technology that they now had at their fingertips mixed with the raw emotions of encroaching "manhood." Hormones run amok, filtered through heavily amped distortion devices, created a guttural howl worthy of mythic warriors—or barbarians. *Led Zeppelin II* was the quintessential LP of this kind of chest-beating stud-rock. Just listen to "Living Loving Maid (She's Just a Woman)," a contemptuous ode to a New Orleans streetwalker featuring a prototypically metallic Page guitar riff; or the lunging "Heartbreaker," which staged its attack in blistering chunks of malevolent fury. Perhaps the most absurd example of Zep's blues bastardizations was "Bring It On Home," which took a standard blues motif—replete with Robert Plant blowing harmonica—and turned it into a hyper-sonic riff of skull-pounding proportions. Page's unique production methods added depth to the proceedings so that the bottom never fell out. Coming as it did at the tail end of the sixties, this album still contains vague psychedelic ("What Is and What Should Never Be") and folk ("Ramble On") traces, but, pound for pound, *Led Zeppelin II* was as "heavy" as it got.   J.S.H.

44

Led Zeppelin

Jimmy Page stepped from the ruins of the Yardbirds looking to do things his way. His former band had led a class of British blues obsessives whose appetite for homage at times made them seem limited in comparison with their psychedelic pop peers. Not so with Page's next band, who would steer the blues into territory that would outstrip all contemporaries for years to come.

Led Zeppelin's debut album doused gasoline on the formerly flickering flame of English blues. Page, a virtuoso with a deep understanding of the recording studio, formed his band with studio pro John Paul Jones. Then Page recruited two unknowns to round out the lineup: monster drummer John Bonham and male Valkyrie Robert Plant. It was a killer combination. Plant wailed like a soul in ecstatic torment, Page played with chaotic precision, and Bonham—well, there was nothing oxymoronic about his abuse of the drum kit. He was simply the heaviest drummer ever.

ATLANTIC
1969
Jimmy Page:
guitars, vocals
Robert Plant:
vocals, harmonica
John Paul Jones:
bass, keyboards,
organ, vocals
John Bonham:
drums, timpani, vocals
Sandy Denny:
vocals
Viram Jasani:
tabla
Produced by
Jimmy Page

Led Zeppelin "borrowed" from traditional blues, but only the most hidebound purist could deny that the record improved on its sources. "You Shook Me" exuded a wholly original raunch and swagger, while the epic "Dazed and Confused" distorted the blues into a psycho-sonic assault that could be compared to Hendrix's best. "Communication Breakdown" was played twice as fast as anything else on the record, was twice as hard, and would be blared from American teenagers' muscle cars for the next decade. The latter song also displayed Page's talent for quick, nasty, almost malevolent guitar solos that stuck in the mind as much as the verses and choruses.

Often overlooked in the wake of the Led Zep assault was their professionalism and their ability to play with nuance and subtlety. Much of this album was acoustic, such as the fingerpicking "Black Mountain Side" and the dynamic "Babe I'm Gonna Leave You." Led Zep played with light and shade, ear-splitting noise and echoing quiet. They could do it all. *Led Zeppelin* captured one of the greatest bands in the universe flexing its muscles for the first time.

Q.S.

Stand!

Before James Brown had really stretched out, Sly Stone was the master of the funk jam—and *Stand!* was the harbinger of extended funk grooves. Sly knew a thing or two about rhythm: Putting the bass up front, and constructing the riffs around a dancing rhythm heavy on stuttering brass and vampy piano, Sly & the Family Stone were the first universal funkhouse, and *Stand!* is the album where they fully transmogrified—and subsequently became one of the most

popular bands in America. In the late sixties and early seventies, Sly achieved the amazing feat of being the only black artist who could compete with the Beatles, Rolling Stones, and Led Zeppelin in the LP market. Sly was the first international black superstar, and the Family was important for being one of the first integrated units. Not only that, but the fact that women participated in the band on the same creative footing as their male counterparts was a huge strike for equality in the mostly male-dominated domain of rock. Carefully melding his outspoken militance with pop sensibilities and rock jamming, Sly achieved the perfect cross-cultural marriage for the era and was rewarded with both commercial and critical success.

His brilliance as an arranger can't be underestimated—the manner in which the piano and horns helped construct the riff on "Everyday People" with seamless chordal progressions was a giant innovation in the field of pop—but there was a darker side as well, as epitomized by the brooding "Don't Call Me Nigger, Whitey," which became an anthem of sorts and has been adapted to rap terms many times. Obviously, Sly & the Family Stone were way ahead of their time, as evidenced by the trippy space-funk purveyed in songs like "Don't Call Me Nigger" and "Sex Machine," which was kind of like the dimension between the psychedelic guitar collages of Hendrix and the roiling jungle-funk of Miles Davis. Sly Stone straddled the stratospheres and American R&B grew up in the process. *Stand!* is a great album from a great innovator.   J.S.H.

> **EPIC**
> 1969
>
> **Sly Stone:**
> vocals, guitar, keyboard
> **Larry Graham:**
> bass, backing vocals
> **Rose Stone:**
> vocals, piano
> **Cynthia Robinson:**
> trumpet, vocals
> **Jerry Martini:**
> saxophone
> **Greg Errico:**
> drums
> **Freddie Stewart:**
> guitar
> **Produced by**
> Sly Stone

Sticky Fingers

<table>
<tr><td colspan="2" align="center">ATLANTIC 1971</td></tr>
<tr><td>Mick Jagger:
vocals</td><td>Charlie Watts:
drums</td></tr>
<tr><td>Keith Richards:
guitar</td><td>Ian Stewart:
piano</td></tr>
<tr><td>Mick Taylor:
guitar</td><td>Bobby Keyes:
saxophone</td></tr>
<tr><td>Bill Wyman:
bass</td><td>Produced by
Jimmy Miller</td></tr>
</table>

Since *Sticky Fingers* was the Rolling Stones' first post-Altamont LP, they more or less made their decision with this album as to whether or not to repent for the sins of that grievous event or continue on the same hellhound trail. Despite the fact that, to many, Altamont was the event that finally capsized the sixties, *Sticky Fingers* showed no remorse for the band's decadent posture. In the next few years, the group would come to epitomize the excesses of the rock-star life, and *Sticky Fingers* was just one way of announcing that to the world. It's surely a laconic LP for a band who,

months before, had railed "Rape, murder / It's just a kiss away." No such foreboding pronouncements characterize *Sticky Fingers*. It is an album of more personal material, and the attitude is drunken laissez-faire. It even came together in a laid-back way. Some tracks dated back to 1969 (including "Brown Sugar" and "Wild Horses"), while others caught the band breaking in new guitarist Mick Taylor, who'd played scantly on the previous album, *Let It Bleed*, but was really just coming into his own as far as being an integrated presence in the band. In short, *Sticky Fingers* was amazingly—and perhaps inadvertently—prescient when it came to predicting what the first half of the seventies would be like.

Taylor's integration into the band can't be underestimated. The Stones had established themselves as a dual-guitar band in the sixties, but for the latter third of the decade, Keith Richards had been pulling the wagon on his own due to Brian Jones having become incapacitated by his indulgences (eventually succumbing to casualty, and then fatality, status). With Taylor in the band, Richards really found his groove, and on numbers like "Brown Sugar," "Sway," "Bitch," and "Can You Hear Me Knockin'," there was a new rocking intensity to the Stones that suggested that the days of "Ruby Tuesday" and other more baroque embellishments were long behind them. This was partly because of Taylor, who was only nineteen when he replaced Jones in the summer of 1969. Taylor had been Eric Clapton's replacement in the Bluesbreakers, so he was no slouch—and while his more fluid style differed greatly from Richards', they flowed together mellifluously.

Once again, almost as if caught between the currents of two different eras, *Sticky Fingers* was also the last Stones LP to demonstrate the brief country flirtation they picked up in the late sixties when Keith Richards became enamored by the American country-rock pioneer Gram Parsons. This influence was most apparent on "Wild Horses" and the rollicking "Dead Flowers," one of the album's best tracks, with Mick singing like a drunken Texan. There was a kind of loose unselfconsciousness that suggested the Stones weren't going to play anyone's martyrs anymore. Soon they would be holed up in a château in France, and Altamont couldn't seem farther away. As always, the blues and R&B influences that had served them so well were still in evidence, in both their cover of the Fred McDowell number "You Gotta Move" as well as in the Memphis soul homage, "I Got the Blues," which might be the most blatant stylistic lift they ever accomplished. Meanwhile, the long jam at the end of "Can You Hear Me Knockin' " dabbled with almost jazzlike improv textures that they simply couldn't have even attempted without Mick Taylor. And "Moonlight Mile," the closer, is an ethereal masterpiece. In fact, in many ways, *Sticky Fingers* showed the group's wide range of talents better than any other album. J.S.H.

Hunky Dory

RCA
1971
David Bowie:
vocals, piano,
saxophone, guitar
Mick Ronson:
guitar
Trevor Bolder:
bass
Mick Woodmanson:
drums
Rick Wakeman:
keyboards
Produced by
Ken Scott

When David Bowie made *Hunky Dory* he was little more than a curiosity in America, probably best known for having come to New York wearing a dress the previous year. Subsequently, on the cover of this album, he struck a similarly androgynous pose. Glam-rock was right around the corner and Bowie would be one of its principle architects, dashing his musical palette with a streak of mascara and putting on trashy airs usually reserved for London West End ingénues and New Orleans streetwalkers. These were the elements that Bowie would help bring to rock, making possible every-thing from punk to Madonna, but in 1971, Bowie was still principally known as yet another Dylanesque folksinger. True, he'd made a futuristic heavy-metal album the year before, with the *Man Who Sold the World*, but as far as the record-buying public was concerned, his only shot at recognition had been a mostly acoustic space-folk ditty entitled "Space Oddity." But people were soon to find out that when it came to David Bowie, expectations were meant to be challenged.

Hunky Dory found Bowie lodged between his initial folk phase and the persona he would soon become. For this reason, it's probably his best album—although surely with an artist like Bowie, whose career has spanned decades and who's dabbled with multiple musical styles, "best" is a relative term. In many ways, *Hunky Dory* was the album in which Bowie began establishing the persona that would make him famous. But in order to do this, he also had to cast off the past, which is why at least three of the songs on *Hunky Dory*—"Song for Bob Dylan," "Andy Warhol," and "Queen Bitch," about Lou Reed—were self-conscious attempts to pay tribute to some of the artists who'd influenced him. This kind of calculated reinvention was also epitomized by the opening track, "Changes," in which Bowie proclaimed "time may change me." He was still sporting a hippie hairdo on the back cover, but in the subsequent years, as Bowie thundered through decadent rock opuses like *The Rise and Fall of Ziggy Stardust*, *Aladdin Sane*, and *Diamond Dogs*, the folkie phase would take a backseat. *Hunky Dory* was his final album to deal with this Dylan-ish fixation, an incarnation that Bowie would always occasionally return to, but never again pursue with as much fervor.

At the same time, the kind of slightly cracked folk-rock epitomized by several tracks on this album wasn't the typical Dylan-strum or country croaking being practiced by many of Bowie's contemporaries (Neil Young, etc.). If anything, Bowie belonged in the category of other eccentric English acid-folkers like Kevin Ayers and Syd Barrett; there was still a hallucinatory quotient, leftover from the sixties. But Bowie was also flamboyantly beckoning the coming age with tracks like "Oh, You Pretty Things" where he sings: "Time to make way for the homo superior."

In many ways, *Hunky Dory* was Bowie's most personal work. Although as an artist Bowie would seldom be accused of earnestness, preferring instead to survive on mystique, performances like "Changes" and "Quicksand" were powerful and convincing. Most importantly, *Hunky Dory* established Bowie as a legitimate long-term talent as opposed to a mere oddity. Bowie, of course, proved eminently capable of handling the fame and adoration while still creating idiosyncratic albums throughout the remainder of the decade. In this sense, *Hunky Dory* can be seen as a catalyst for one of the most enduring careers in rock.   J . S . H .

The Rise and Fall of Ziggy Stardust

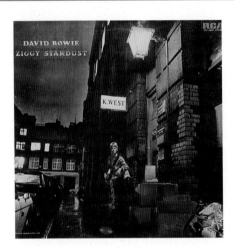

David Bowie is probably the single most influential vocalist and songwriter on me. It's not just his voice, which I think is just a rich tone of gold, but his ability to write lyrics and his overall class, style, and grace.

—SCOTT WEILAND

By 1972 David Bowie had spent more than five years chasing trends and waiting for the world to catch up with his perception of himself. He had honed his craft and come up with a unique mix of paranoia and whimsy the year before on *Hunky Dory*, but he was by no means a fixture in the rock firmament.

There was only one logical thing to do: scramble his mind and adopt the persona of an androgynous, sex-crazed messianic space alien.

It worked. His songwriting came into sharp focus, his voice took on unexpected immediacy,

and, with guitarist Mick Ronson, he formulated a dramatic, melodic style that carried the wistful longing and strange fancies of the character he was to inhabit. *Ziggy Stardust* inaugurated a period of stunning artistic achievement for Bowie that lasted through the decade.

Ziggy kicks off with "Five Years," an apocalyptic drama that sets the tone for what's to come. From the freaky "Moonage Daydream" to the youthful romance of "Soul Love," this LP's greatness resides largely in the mood it evokes—one in which all things are new, with the passion and hunger of youth recast as an end-all in a world of sci-fi futurism.

Some have tagged *Ziggy* with the dread "concept album" label, but listeners need not fear lengthy exposition or filler tracks that strain to tell a story. The reality of *Ziggy* is like the glossy sheen of a Dali painting—all texture and surface, with a deranged heart beating underneath. In assuming a character, Bowie liberated himself to write without conscience. Ziggy the alien was an apocalyptic hedonist and a lascivious "leper messiah" for the End Days. The "story" of Ziggy was, in fact, an answer to the incomplete emancipation of Flower Power, an imaginary world of the soul in which the young were exhorted to love who they wished, how they wished, in a world of glamor and gadgetry, and to do it as though there were no tomorrow.

The outrageous Ziggy image tended to obscure the fact that Bowie made some of the best straight-ahead rock 'n' roll of his career on this album, and that his voice never sounded better. The LP's title track, all crunching guitars

VIRGIN
1972
David Bowie:
guitar, keyboards, sax, vocals
Trevor Bolder:
bass
Mick Ronson:
guitar, piano, vocals
Rick Wakeman:
keyboards
Mick "Woody" Woodmansey:
drums
Dana Gillespie:
background vocals
Produced by
David Bowie, Ken Scott

and high drama—in which Ziggy sings about Ziggy, in a brilliant mind-warp—would stick in rock's collective craw.

The LP ends with "Rock and Roll Suicide," in which Ziggy implodes under the weight of his own ego. The song verges on the ridiculous, but an album of such boldness and dramatic indulgence demands nothing less. *Ziggy* closes with Bowie, over rising strings, telling his audience "you're wonderful" in a voice transported with ecstasy. It's a hall of mirrors, in which an artist who has taken refuge behind a dramatic persona ostensibly bestows a benediction of communion upon his yearning, clamoring fans. Was it real, was it an act? And what was the difference, anyway?

Bowie would later say that *Ziggy* was hard to shake, that the alien messiah love god had taken hold in his consciousness and didn't want to go away. Small wonder. *Ziggy Stardust* is the main document of one of rock's great philosophical and artistic experiments. Q.S.

1999

WARNER BROS.
1983
Prince:
vocals, guitars,
keyboards, bass, drums
Wendy Melvoin:
guitar, percussion, vocals
Lisa Coleman:
keyboards, vocals
Dez Dickerson:
guitar, vocals
Brownmark:
bass, vocals
Produced by
Prince

By 1983, Prince had already shown himself to be a major talent. Pop watchers agreed that his skills as a singer, songwriter, multi-instrumentalist, and producer were comparable to those of his idol, Stevie Wonder. Unlike Wonder, though, Prince had remained more or less a cult artist. Catchy as early albums like *Dirty Mind* and *Controversy* were, their explicit content scared off many potential listeners. It seemed that as long as Prince continued to focus on such subjects as fellatio and ménages à trois, he would never reach a higher level of stardom. Then

along came *1999*, a landmark double album on which Prince maintained his wanton ways while pushing his music just close enough to the mainstream to garner a well-deserved commercial breakthrough.

The song that made it all happen was "Little Red Corvette," a clever exploitation of the time-honored link between fast cars and hot sex. This salaciously hissed tale of a loose woman and her favorite vehicle strayed close to the single-entendre line—"She had a pocketful of horses/ Trojans, some of them used," for example—

and, mumble though he might, it was still pretty obvious that Prince was singing, "Girl, you got an ass like I never seen." But the big rock chorus and heroic guitar solo made prudish resistance futile. "Little Red Corvette" was plainly designed for crossover success, which was just what it achieved, winning Prince a new—and primarily white—audience.

Not much else on *1999* sounded like "Little Red Corvette." Most of the album's tracks were extended pieces of sparse robo-funk, with synthesizers and drum machines comprising the main sonic components. As on his previous releases, Prince handled the recording responsibilites and nearly all the instruments; the Revolution, the band with which he recorded *Purple Rain* and *Around the World in a Day*, among others, was not yet formed (although the words "and the Revolution" are scrawled in tiny letters on *1999*'s cover, and several future group members make cameo appearances). But the overtly mechanical beats on songs like "Something in the Water (Does Not Compute)" and "D.M.S.R."—that's "dance, music, sex, romance," in case you were wondering—marked fresh territory for the diminutive

rocker. Far from sounding stiff, they were mesmerizing, and they made you want to get up and move.

The audience won over by "Little Red Corvette" apparently wasn't alienated by this strange new sound, since two more songs on *1999* became huge hits as well: the ubiquitous title cut, an exuberant ode to apocalypse, and "Delirious," a bouncy blues with a distinctive synth-squiggle riff. Just as infectious but more risqué were "International Lover," a lusty ballad that made novel use of air-travel terminology, and "Lady Cab Driver," in which our hero violently forces himself on the titular subject while musing about Yosemite Sam.

Yet the album's key track, and the clearest window into Prince's unique world view, was "Let's Pretend We're Married." For the first several minutes, it's a straightforward do-me number ("Come on, baby, let's ball" is one line); then it takes a sharp turn to the right with a closing mass chant about God and the afterlife. Puzzling? Sure. But in the end, the insistent groove is all that matters. Which is why, even as the year 1999 fades into history, the album *1999* is still a party favorite.   M . R .

Synchronicity

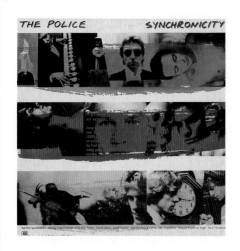

I'd say that was a pretty good note to go out on. Say we trudged on for another seven or eight years and our albums would be staying at 64 on the *Billboard* charts. That wouldn't have been a good time to leave. In fact, we got off at the top of the curve. In some ways it was a brilliant time to wave good-bye.

—ANDY SUMMERS

Life is made up of serendipity, and one of my life's favorites is that my older sister was a fanatical devotee of the Police when we were growing up. To this day, I know the lyrics to nearly all of the British band's songs—all because a constant stream of Police music would flow from my sister's bedroom (which was, of course, wallpapered with photos and posters of Sting, Stewart Copeland and Andy Summers).

Though Sting has long since settled into his adult contemporary Barcalounger, the Police were, once upon a time, a punk band. Though they'd released a total of four albums leading up to *Synchronicity*, it was this fifth album that would show them as a true pop-culture force with which to be reckoned.

Propelled by the smash-hit single, "Every Breath You Take," 1983 became the year of the Police. The single caught fire, thanks, in part, to a heavily rotated video on then-nascent MTV. It has since been named one of the biggest singles of all time, and who could forget the Puff Daddy version, which—much to the shock and chagrin of many of his fans—

bore Sting-approved samples of the song.

While *Synchronicity* didn't debut at number one on the U.S. charts, it didn't take long to get there—holding on tight to the spot for seventeen weeks straight, setting a record for most consecutive weeks at number one. The album has since been certified platinum eight times.

For all its record-breaking prowess, *Synchronicity* isn't necessarily strong because every single song on it is a hit. Songs like "Walking in Your Footsteps" verge on ridiculous, while Andy Summers's vocals on "Mother"—one I'd always beg my sister to fast-forward through—are akin to fingernails on a chalkboard. In other words: *Synchronicity* is almost more of a success story because it was able to overcome such apparent shortcomings.

That said, *Synchronicity* obviously isn't without its high points. For starters, many of its songs showcase Sting's erudite songwriting—it's clear all of his years of being an English teacher paid off in the passages that quote Greek mythology ("Wrapped Around Your Fin-

UNI/A&M
1983
Sting:
vocals, bass
Andy Summers:
guitar, vocals
Stewart Copeland:
drums, vocals
Produced by
Hugh Padgham

ger") and Scottish fairy tales ("Synchronicity II"). I'll always credit the Police as having educated me on the story behind Mephistopheles, not to mention pointing me in the direction of Jungian philosophy.

Of all the weighty references the album makes—the title being but one of them—it's "Synchronicity II"'s stunningly apt portral of a day in the life of a dysfunctional, middle-American family that really stands out in my mind. Like a female novelist writing in the male voice, Sting—a Brit through and through—is able to astutely and poetically capture the idiosyncrasies of banal, suburban Stateside life. Who knew the mundane could be so damn poignant?

When all is said and done, *Synchronicity* will always stand out in my mind (and doubtless others') as one of the albums that proved that intelligence and pop music didn't have to be mutually exclusive. With this album, the Police raised the bar and provided a benchmark to which pop lyricists have since aspired, but rarely achieved. — C.R.

Dark Side of the Moon

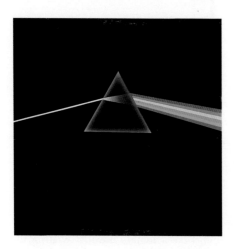

For years I've been arguing that *Dark Side of the Moon* is the best rock album ever, with the emphasis on album. Because, while there are a few albums that contain more and better individual songs, with *Dark Side of the Moon*, Pink Floyd produced a fully realized, coherent work of art. As such, it is just about perfect.

The iconographic cover art says it all: A prism breaks light down into its component colors. In critical theory, the fracture of light represents the fall of man—from grace to sin, from one language to many, from pure, sacred light to the earth's many colors. In songs such as "Money," "Us and Them," and "Time," Pink Floyd break down and explore the greed, division, and ignorance of our own mortality that contribute to our personal falls. Whether intentional or not, the image contributes to the sense that this album is the product of a band in complete aesthetic control.

That control extends to the writing. The always astute lyrics of Roger Waters find the perfect harmony of intellectual-ism and melodrama. "And the General sat, and the lines on the map moved from side to side."

The songs are simple, primal, and uncluttered. But they seem to contain worlds. The lyrics, despite tackling such heady themes, are refreshingly devoid of self-consciousness. They flow simply and naturally, as rhymes like "no one told you when to run / you missed the starting gun" fold into one another organically.

And, oh yes, the music: phenomenal. Few if any albums sound better, but *Dark Side of the Moon's* strength is not only found in the atmospherics and superb stereo reproduction. The band rocks, with David Gilmour, in particular, putting in spectacular performances on guitar and vocals. If the last time you listened to this album was on your teenage stereo, you ought to go back to it on your adult sound system, and use it to test your speakers' tolerances.

CAPITOL
1973

David Gilmour:
guitar, keyboards, VCS 3 synthesizer, vocals

Roger Waters:
bass, guitar, keyboards, VCS 3 synthesizer, vocals

Richard Wright:
keyboards, VCS 3 synthesizer, vocals

Nick Mason:
drums, percussion

Dick Parry:
saxophone

Claire Torry:
vocals

Lesley Duncan, Liza Strike, Doris Troy:
background vocals

Produced by
Pink Floyd

Though few albums seem better suited to the promise of CD sound quality, *Dark Side of the Moon* is actually one of those LPs that loses something when its two sides become one. Each side of the original record was a voyage that ended on a high peak—side A with the psychedelic gospel of "Great Gig in the Sky" and side B with the triumphant "Eclipse," ("Everything under the sun is in tune, but the sun is eclipsed by the moon.") The album as a whole is also one big loop. It goes out where it came in, with a heartbeat, which seems appropriate for what may be rock's most successful meditation on the human condition.

It also makes a great soundtrack to the opening forty-three minutes of *The Wizard of Oz.*

Note: If interested in pursuing this, to best sync up the movie with the music, you will need to press play on the third roar from the famous MGM lion. Enjoy.

E.W.

The Pretenders

Despite the Year One pretensions of the late seventies English punk bands, the best music from the British Isles has always been strong on melody and song craft (John Lydon, after all, claims today that he and the Sex Pistols were great ABBA fans. 1980 saw the release of the Clash's *London Calling*, no slouch in the tunes department, and the Pretenders, one of the strongest debuts in music history.

Ohio exile Chrissie Hynde had been in the trenches of Punk since its murky mid-seventies inception, playing in bands and writing record reviews. She played in a variety of nascent groups and configurations, watching her friends go on to success with groups such as the Damned and the aforementioned Clash. Probably fearing a jilted-at-the-altar trajectory to her music career, she slogged away and recorded a demo that earned her a manager and the wherewithal to audition a band.

And here was the thing about Chrissie Hynde: she was rough, she was raw, and her voice was almost unbelievably great. She had great bangs, she wore leather, and she stared at the camera as though she would just as soon punch it into shards as pose for it. She was a star waiting to happen. Matter were helped along when James Honeyman-Scott joined up. Rather than a journeyman punker, he was a throwback obsessed with technique and effects, and who took his musical cues as much from sixties pop as from seventies anarchy. Bassist Pete Farndon and drummer Martin Chambers added a solid base to the new band's sound.

The Pretenders revealed an original talent rife with contradictions. The songs shot a middle finger to the world with the aggro opener "Precious," then later applied honeyed voice and shimmering guitar to the Kinks cover "Stop Your Sobbing." American audiences caught on to "Brass in Pocket," a chiming, chugging number that featured an aching sensual vocal that some found hard to imagine emerging from the apparently disheveled and perpetually pissed-off Hynde. But that was what made it all so interesting—Hynde's vacillations between the crude come-ons of "Tattoed Love Boys" and the tear-stained tenderness of "Kid." She could not be categorized easily, nor her talent demonstrated in a single composition. She was a natural, and even the lesser songs on the LP sparkle with the life and possibility of a great band still learning how to play together.

The record goes out like a champion, with the sulky "Lovers of Today" followed by the percussive thrust and dynamic vocals on "Mystery Achievement." The Pretenders had managed to fire off about seven songs full of undeniable greatness that still sound relevant and contemporary almost a quarter-century later. It was a high-water moment for Hynde's band, but hard times were soon to come—after a very good second album, with several more standout tracks, the original band line-up imploded. Within two years half of the group would be dead. Some great tunes followed, well into the nineties, as Hynde alternately mellowed and rocked hard again as the years passed. No matter the quality of later efforts, though, the Pretenders debut remains the band's lasting accomplishment. Q.S.

Bringing It All Back Home

In the annals of rock mythology, *Bringing It All Back Home* is the album on which Bob Dylan left protest singing behind and went electric. Rock mythology being what it is, neither of those claims are accurate. Dylan's first record without a protest song was *Another Side of Bob Dylan*, released in 1964, and he'd recorded with an electric band as early as 1962. Yet, nitpicking aside, *Bringing It All Back Home* undeniably marks a major change in Dylan's career. If not the birth of a new Dylan, it's at least a bold announcement that the old one has risen to a higher level, his music and lyrics feeding off each other to achieve an unprecedented intensity.

Before he became a leading light on the New York folk scene, Dylan had been a rocker. He'd grown up adoring Elvis, Buddy Holly, and the many other rebel heroes who scandalized American society in the fifties. By going electric, Dylan really was bringing it all back home, to what had inspired him to play music in the first place. But even Chuck Berry and Eddie Cochran at their most imaginative had never come close to the verbal frenzy of "Subterranean Homesick

53

Blues," which opens *Bringing It All Back Home* in appropriately brazen fashion. As the band bashes out a loud, ragged 12 bars, Dylan spits out one rapid-fire line after another with his trademark nasal whine, touching on everything from government paranoia to advertising cliches to what seemed like coded generational advice ("Don't follow leaders, watch the parking meters"). He's part Beat poet, part prophet, part stand-up comedian, and all rock 'n' roll.

If the sheer volume of Dylan's new songs wasn't enough to clue you in that his folkie days were over, you could just read between the lines. On "She Belongs to Me," he equates being an artist with not looking back. On "Outlaw Blues," he hints that those who ask him questions aren't really interested in the truth. And on "Maggie's Farm," he rails, "I try my best to be just like I am / But everybody wants you to be just like them," a remark that aimed straight for both Dylan's colleagues and his audience.

All these songs appear on *Bringing It All Back*

COLUMBIA
1965
Bob Dylan:
vocals, guitar, harmonica
Bruce Langhorne:
guitar
Paul Griffin:
piano
Bobby Gregg:
drums
Various additional musicians

Produced by
Tom Wilson

Home's first half, along with the pretty, enigmatic ballad "Love Minus Zero/No Limit" and one of Dylan's most hilarious narratives, "Bob Dylan's 115th Dream." But absorbing as side one was, it was the quieter, nearly all-acoustic side two that offered the greatest evidence of Dylan's growth. "Mr. Tambourine Man," "Gates of Eden," "It's Alright, Ma (I'm Only Bleeding)," and "It's All Over Now, Baby Blue" are nonstop explosions of hallucinatory imagery, as elusive as they are allusive. Who is Mr. Tambourine Man? What are curfew gulls? What does Dylan mean when he sings, "There are no truths outside the gates of Eden"? From queries like these arose an entire Dylan explication industry, which continues its relentless parsing to this day.

The man who wrote the songs provided no answers. He touted no causes. He meant whatever you thought he meant. And on *Bringing It All Back Home,* he proves definitively that what a song means doesn't matter much. What matters is that it makes you feel.   M . R .

Ramones

Here it is—the album that split the history of rock 'n' roll in half, New Testament, Old Testament. Those who heard—I mean, really heard—the fourteen bracing numbers that make up *Ramones* upon its release in 1976 knew that rock would never be the same again. To the generation of fans and musicians who would come to constitute something known as "punk rock," this album provided the same shock of recognition that the Beatles had for the previous musical generation. It's impossible to think of a rock band in the postpunk era that wasn't influenced by the

Ramones. Despite being shunned by the industry and dismissed by the critics, the Ramones were a force to be reckoned with. And excited rock fans, stuck in the absolute malaise of the ultra-lame mid-seventies, understood that instantly.

The sounds heard on the Ramones' first album all had their antecedents. The lunging chord structure and fuzzed-out attack of Johnny Ramone's guitar was clearly influenced by seventies heavy-metal bands like Black Sabbath, as well as proto-punk precursors like the Stooges. Meanwhile, the melodic simplicity of songs like

54

SIRE
1976
Joey Ramone:
vocals
Johnny Ramone:
guitar
Dee Dee Ramone:
bass
Tommy Ramone:
drums
Produced by
Craig Leon

"Blitzkrieg Bop," as well as the throbbing beat, came straight from late-sixties bubblegum, the Beach Boys, and other rock 'n' roll oldies. One could even make a claim that their insistence on wearing a uniform—ripped jeans, T-shirts, and leather jackets, in this case—was an ironic nod to the Beatles' patented moptops and gray suits. The Ramones arrived at that weird juncture in the culture when "retro" itself was a whole new concept (i.e., *Happy Days*, etc.). But the difference between the Ramones and contemporaneous bands like the Rubinoos was that the Ramones made reference to the past ironically—like the fact that, although they were Jewish, they did songs with titles like "Blitzkrieg Bop" and "Today Your Love, Tomorrow the World," and that they used the poppy melodies to construct odes to glue sniffing and first degree murder. This was the "punk" part and that was what stuck.

When it came out, the first thing one noticed was the cranking tempo. Playing at a breakneck pace that, at that time, was unprecedented, the Ramones created a kind of static hum that lobbed across the placid mid-seventies rock tableau like a torpedo. And lyrically, although the Ramones might have addressed negative issues, they didn't necessarily sound unhappy. It was a weird new kind of urban ethos that summed up the times a lot better than the Captain and Tennille (although that was what was on the radio at the time). Hippies complained about the violent content, missing the joke entirely. And arena- and art-rock snobs scoffed at the simplicity of it all, mistakenly believing that the Ramones were "dumb." But as drummer/executive producer Tommy Ramone said in a *Rolling Stone* interview in 1979: "If every untrained musician doing the best he can decides to make a record, he's not going to get a Ramones LP out of it."

What the Ramones were doing was reestablishing the precedent of the original rock pioneers like Bo Diddley and Jimmy Reed, who utilized simplistic and sometimes repetitious formulas to create profound changes in the fabric of American music. In this sense, *Ramones* is one of the most groundbreaking albums of all time.　J.S.H.

Mothership Connection

UNI/MERCURY 1976

George Clinton:
vocals

Bootsy Collins:
bass, drums, guitar,
percussion, vocals

Cordell Mosson:
bass

Bernie Worrell:
keyboards,
synthesizer

Glen Goins,
Michael Hampton,
Gary Shider:
guitar

Jerome Brailey,
Gary "Muddbone"
Cooper, Ramon
Tiki Fulwood:
drums, percussion

Michael Brecker,
Randy Brecker,
Joe Farrell,
Maceo Parker,
Fred Wesley:
horns

Raymond Davis,
Clarence
"Fuzzy" Haskins,
Calvin Simon,
Grady Thomas:
vocals

Produced by
George Clinton

There was a time when the citizens of America's Chocolate Cities—Detroit, Atlanta, D.C.—found themselves in dire need of liberation. They turned to the Star Child, who came down in the mothership to make things funky and take them home. He arrived bearing the gift of da funk, and he blessed them with the immortal wisdom: "Free your mind and your ass will follow."

Such was George Clinton's vision in the seventies. Clinton had put in time as a doo-wop singer and staff writer for Motown, but his unshakeable weirdness necessitated a break from the acceptable norms

of R&B. Clinton established himself as the focal point of the Parliament-Funkadelic nexus, a collection of refugees from top soul bands who joined forces to release a staggering collection of records. P-Funk captivated the imagination of African Americans in the seventies, creating a powerful mythology and a soundtrack for the best parties.

In 1976, Parliament would release two albums, and so would Funkadelic. These were not compilations or tossed-off efforts (those would come later), but full-fledged band efforts. Of these, *Mothership Connection* is the best. It's all here—Bootsy Collins's elastic bass, Bernie Worrell's extraterrestrial synthesizers, Gary Shider's guitar, Fred Wesley's horny horns. And, laid on top of it all, are George Clinton's vocals—teasing, mocking, exhorting, and celebrating, with a worldview that melded W. E. B. Du Bois with a Marvel superhero comic.

The album kicks off with "P-Funk (Wants to Get Funked Up)," which follows the pattern of all great P-Funk anthems—layered horns, guitars, and synths wending over an airtight rhythmic bed. It is a relentless tune, with lyrics ("Make my funk the P-Funk") evoking a sort of national craze for da funk. It was a self-fulfilling prophesy, for although P-Funk had enjoyed success before 1976, this would be the year when they ruled as one of the most popular bands in America.

Mothership Connection, like all the best P-Funk LPs, does not let up. The title track throws out a rhythmic curveball, "Give Up the Funk (Tear the Roof Off the Sucker)," that tickles the ear with dense, layered sound, and "Night of the Thumpasorus Peoples" lumbers with a deep, dark groove. This is music to put on when you want your party to shift into the next gear, for it is next to impossible to sit still while it is playing. P-Funk always subscribed to the notion that more was better, and stuck to it: Polyrhythmic beats and multiple vocal tracks fight for attention in the same groove, pulling the mind and booty in several directions at once. *Mothership Connection* never sounds the same way twice.

Mothership Connection appeals to anyone who loves music, though in its time it was created as part of a distinctly African American phenomenon. P-Funk reflected adult African American sensibilities and concerns, and was wildly popular as a result. Parliament hit big because of their hardcore funky grooves, but their imagery and ethos were essential. On *Mothership Connection*, George Clinton evokes his starship with the stunning co-opting of the line "swing low, sweet chariot," and ties together centuries of African American suffering under a transcendent wish for release, for freedom, for happiness—in short, for da funk. In "Chocolate City," the year before, he had reminded his audience that they were the residents of American cities surrounded by "vanilla suburbs," that they were America. P-Funk celebrated blackness, celebrated life, and managed to do it with a nudge, a leer, and an order from Uncle Jam to move your ass.   Q.S.

Trans-Europe Express

Visions of robots, synthesizers, and metallic objects must have danced around in the minds of Depeche Mode's Martin Gore, Gary Numan, Erasure's Vince Clarke, Ultravox, and countless other future electro craftsmen. Those symbolic and Moog-moving images were provided by the constructive conductors of "Robot Pop," Kraftwerk. While the group unleashed its machinery mastermind with former albums, *Kraftwerk 1*, *Kraftwerk 2*, *Ralf and Florian*, *Autobahn* (which provided the Top 25 single of the same name), and *Radio-Activity*, the album that clanged and charged its way into the hearts of synthboppers and early hip-hop pioneers was *Trans-Europe Express.*

When *Trans-Europe Express* was released, it was not only the heyday of punk and disco, but also, in Europe especially, the heyday of Abba!. Kraftwerk absorbed all of these influences and combined them with their own technocratic art-rock impulses in a fresh manner that helped obliterate the facade prevalent in seventies arena-rock, that the synthesizer was only for arty purposes. Along with Giorgio Moroder, another German who was experimenting with such techniques at the same time, Kraftwerk helped turn the synthesizer into a pop-making device. Whereas before, their recordings had consisted mostly of a Morse code–like dialogue between Ralf and Florian, on *Trans-Europe Express*, they'd turned the synthesizers into a total environment of whooshing sweeping wholeness.

Leading the slow but steady journey out of the station, is the melancholy yet eerily beautiful landscaped "Europe Endless." Here, you can envision a student's first trip across Europe, clutching a Euro-rail pass and soaking in the images of never-before-seen mountains, castles, and countryside. Next stop on the high-speed head-trip is a narcissistic view in "The Hall of Mirrors." With Flash Gordon–like sound effects, and shoe-drop pounds, Kraftwerk conveys that "even the greatest stars find their face in the looking glass," only to find unhappiness with their own reflection. Simply put, Kraftwerk creates a grim undertone to a glamorous existence.

In "Showroom Dummies," Gregorian chants

CAPITOL
1977
Ralf Hutter:
synthesizer
Florian Schneider:
synthesizer
Karl Bartos:
electronic percussion,
percussion
Wolfgang Flur:
electronic percussion,
synthesizer, percussion
Produced by
Kraftwerk

vibrate as the staccato synthesizer invokes images of store mannequins breaking through store windows to escape to the city and club life. Kraftwerk could easily have written a few episodes for Rod Serling's *Twilight Zone* with their waxing ways in this simplistic song.

In Germany, 1977, little did Ralf, Karl, Florian, and Wolfgang know that the title track would go on to be the driving force behind New York City pop-lockers on vinyl linoleum in future Afrika Bambaataa's electro-funk classic, "Planet Rock." That combination of synthesizer and funk hip-hop would continue as a trend for years.

The three titles that complete the trip are "Metal on Metal," "Franz Schubert," and "Endless Endless," all instrumental passages that leave the listener contemplating the trip on which they've just been taken. Kraftwerk laid the tracks for all future "liquid engineers" who are welcome to ride the rails of "Trans-Europe Express."

"Liquid Engineers"—Taken from Gary Numan's "Metal." R.B.

57 Saturday Night Fever

A gritty commentary on urban escapism and class struggle, *Saturday Night Fever* follows the ever-cool Tony Manero (John Travolta) from the backstreets of Brooklyn to the nightclubs of Manhattan on a quest for dance-floor supremacy and social dignity. In striking contrast, an ebullient string of now-classic DJ faves like "Night Fever," "Jive Talkin'," and, of course, "Stayin' Alive" provide devil-may-care bravado and hip-grinding groove to the rush of raw images. The film and soundtrack effectively ushered the disco era into the mainstream and helped make household names out of Barry, Maurice, and Robin Gibb, better known as the Bee Gees. Decked out in tight white pants and open polyester shirts revealing carefully preened chest hair, the brothers' saccharine vocal harmonies and irresistibly catchy melodies helped the *Saturday Night Fever* double LP become the biggest-selling soundtrack of all time.

This tremendous success spawned a second wind for the Bee Gees' career. Though they had scored a number of hits in the late sixties, the Australian pop fraternity's popularity had been waning. Then they recorded "Jive Talkin'," a syncopated bump 'n' grind anthem, which gave them their first number-one hit in the United States and revived the public's interest in a vocal group who had previously been known for their goody-two-shoes image and ditties like "New York Mining Disaster 1941" and "Lonely Days." With this change in artistic direction bringing them newfound levels of popularity, their manager Robert Stigwood decided the group would be the perfect music overseers of his most recent project, a film adaptation of a *Vanity Fair* article, "Tribal Rites of the New Saturday Night." The brothers ended up writing half the album and recording six tunes, three of which would end up hitting the top slot on the American charts, and would help them win a brace of Grammys for the mantel.

Thirty years later, everybody still aspires to be as swaggery as Tony Manero, even as the songs of *Saturday Night Fever* remain perennial favorites and ensure that the Bee Gees will not be forgotten anytime soon.   N.M.

POLYDOR RECORDS
1977
Robin Gibb:
vocals
Maurice Gibb:
vocals
Barry Gibb:
vocals
Various musicians

Produced by
Robert Stigwood

Dusty in Memphis

Dusty in Memphis may not have been a chart-topping album, and indeed contains only one of Dusty Springfield's hits, "Son of a Preacher Man." Yet it's a classic, coupling one of the great vocal stylists of her time (who died of breast cancer in 1999) with the Memphis studio pros who backed stars from Wilson Pickett to Otis Redding to another iconic white-person-with-soul, Elvis Presley (who released an *In Memphis* of his own that year).

The album was something of a comeback vehicle, an attempt at self-reinvention. Springfield was best known for singing—as she put it herself in the original liner notes—"big ballady things." but her hits, "I Only Want to Be with You," "Stay Awhile," "You Don't Have to Say You Love Me," etc., had all been cut earlier in the decade. By 1969, she was a mascaraed refugee from the black-and-white world of the British Invasion who didn't quite mesh with late sixties giants like Led Zeppelin and Janis Joplin.

Memphis wouldn't solve that relevance problem. Instead it matches

WEA
1969

Dusty Springfield:
vocals

The Sweet Inspirations:
background vocals

Bobby Wood:
piano

Reggie Young:
guitar, sitar

Gene Chrisman:
drums

Tommy Cogbill:
bass

Tom Dowd:
horn

Bobby Emmons:
conga, organ, piano

Mike Leach:
conga

Produced by
Jeff Barry

her with some of the great songwriters of the period—Goffin/King, Mann/Weil, Bacharach/David, Randy Newman—in a swampy, R&B setting. (Ironically enough, she ended up recording most of her vocals in New York.) Springfield had a unique voice—"Smoky, sexy, restrained, smoldering," recalled Burt Bacharach in a BBC-TV special about her life—that could pack an emotional punch without ever overwhelming the listener.

In fact, there was always something a little unknowable about Dusty Springfield, something that, like her sexuality, she hid. "Never let yourself be too get-at-able," the singer once said. And she never did. You can listen to this album over and over and discover new layers of feeling in the vocals, or just enjoy the ménage of twangy guitars, big-studio string arrangements, and Brill Building song craft. *Dusty in Memphis* is a monument to a previous golden era in pop that transcends retro cool and achieves a sublime timelessness.   S.C.

At Fillmore East

Long before crowds of ribald southern-fried rock music fans exhorted "Free Bird!" they screamed "Whipping Post" at Dixie's original southern boogie band, the Allman Brothers. Long before Lynyrd Skynyrd crawled out of the gator swamps of Florida, the Allmans were the prototypes for the bluesy jams, gruff vocalizings, and whipping guitar jams that came to characterize "southern rock." This was no surprise since brothers Duane and Gregg had been in some kind of band since their teens, and Duane had already earned a rep as one of the leading session men in the south,

making his presence known on a handful of recordings by artists such as Aretha Franklin and Wilson Pickett recorded at the nexus of southern music-making, Muscle Shoals. It's no lie to say that Duane Allman might have been America's greatest white blues guitarist at that time, and the Allman Brothers were part of the blues revival in the U.S. that also included bands like Canned Heat and the J. Geils Band.

Initially the blues revival was a move away from psychedelia, but what the Allmans carried from that era was the concept of the endless jam, which they partly borrowed from the Grateful Dead—the fact that the Allmans, like the Dead, employed two drummers was further testament to the fact that they were attempting the same kind of organic chemistry. But the Allmans proved to be far more capable of sustaining a lasting groove, as *At Fillmore East* proves. Recorded in late 1970 over a few nights where the band jammed til dawn during one of their legendary runs at Bill Graham's Fillmore East, this album is the epitome of stoned sixties jamming: with tracks like "Whipping Post" and "In Memory of Elizabeth Reed" running over twenty minutes, it's obvious that the band were striving for an almost jazz-like level of improvisational briliance. It's to their credit—and producer Tom Dowd, who edited several performances into a seamless mosaic—that they pulled it off with both soul and finesse. "Statesboro Blues" is scalding hot blues with a little of that redneck nastiness that Gregg Allman was good at. Speaking of blues, they also do the best interpretation *ever* of T-Bone Walker's

ATCO
1971
Duane Allman:
guitar
Dickey Betts:
guitar
Gregg Allman:
vocals, piano
Berry Oakley:
bass
Butch Trucks:
drums
Jaimoe Johanny Johnson:
drums
Produced by
Tom Dowd

"Stormy Monday." But it's the embryonic jamming of "Whipping Post," the encore, that really seals this album's fate—this is what the band would become famous for, an endless climb of heightening drama staked out by the twin-guitar exorcisms of Duane and Dickey Betts and the cool, measured, almost jazz-like response of the rhythm section. It was a formula they'd take even further with the next LP, *Eat a Peach*, where a single performance of "Mountain Jam" would spread over two sides.

Unfortunately Duane wouldn't live to see its release, dying tragically in a motorcycle accident just as *At Fillmore East* was turning the band into legends in their own time. In a macabre twist of fate, bassist Berry Oakley would die in the same manner, in almost the same spot, almost exactly a year later. As tragic as this incident was, it only increased the band's image as authentic hellhound-on-my-trail bluesmen. As *At Fillmore East* proves, it was a legend they earned. J . S . H .

The Doors

Even those who love the Doors can go back and forth about their place in the rock and roll canon, but about their first, self-titled album there can be no doubt: *The Doors* bears the mark of greatness and must surely rank as one of the most impressive debuts in rock history. Sadly, it may also have represented the band's creative peak.

But I have come here to praise the Doors, not to bury them. And even if their short, uneven career as a band is ultimately to be judged a disappointment, it is only because it showed so very much promise at the outset. That promise, embodied in *The Doors*, was of an excellent group of musicians who, for the first time in rock, fused theater, psychedelia, urban darkness, and a genuine—if, at times, sophomoric—intellectual sensibility. To hear this album is to hear the birth of art rock—especially the strain that would become Goth.

Even today, more than thirty-five years after *The Doors* was released, the album retains its edge. From the first bars of "Break On Through (To the Other Side)" to its definitive, side two finish ("This . . . is . . . the . . . ehhhhhhuhhnnnnd"), it's an edge maintained by the group's close attention to dynamics and its awareness of what you can do in music when you alternate restraint with release. The band bridges these extremes with a core sound that seems uniquely suited to the task of building and maintaining tension—Ray Manzarek's aggressively innovative keyboard playing high in the mix, Robby Krieger's sinuous and subtle guitar, and John Densmore's tight, punctuating drum figures. And yes, that voice: Jim Morrison may or may not have been a poet, a clown, or a holy fool. He was, though, most assuredly a *singer*.

The rock vernacular embraced a range of vocal styles by the late 1960s; crooner, however was not among them, and a crooner is essentially what Jim Morrison was. His remains one of the most distinctive voices in popular music, by turns lusty and growling, tender and grand. On *The Doors,* as elsewhere in the Doors's recordings, Morrison's ability to really put a song over is readily evident. He had the ability to make a pop confection like "Twentieth Century Fox"

ELEKTRA
1967
Jim Morrison:
vocals
Ray Manzarek:
organ, piano, bass
Robby Krieger:
guitar
John Densmore:
drums
Produced by
Paul A. Rothchild

sound menacing and mysterious, and to render palatable heavier pieces that few others could pull off (try to imagine just about anyone else singing "The End," and you'll get the picture). Morrison sang with *authority*, and it's a quality that allowed the Doors to explore the poles of such apposite covers as Brecht-Weill's quirky "Alabama Song (Whiskey Bar)" and Willie Dixon's leering "Back Door Man." It also made the band's weaker material, such as "Take It as It Comes" and "I Looked at You" on this album, interesting nonetheless.

The legend of the Doors sits heavy on their musical legacy, like the bloated, whiskey-gutted character Morrison became in his later days. At the heart of this legacy, though, are driving, literate, expertly played rock and roll songs—songs that infused their albums with palpable strangeness, sexiness, and bite. Songs that gave backbone and substance to Morrison's lizard king caricature. In no place in the Doors's catalog do they hit harder than on this groundbreaking first album.   E.W.

Crosby, Stills, Nash & Young
Dallas Taylor & Greg Reeves

Déjà vu

Déjà vu

61

"We all felt very strongly about our own ability to contribute, but we thought that Neil was just too good to pass up." That's David Crosby's explanation for why, with three singer-songwriters in Crosby, Stills & Nash, the group decided to invite a fourth—Neil Young—to join. "And I think we were right."

With their track record at that point, CSN were smart to trust their instincts. Their debut album was an instant classic and showed that all three members would have an artistic life after leaving their respective bands: the Byrds (Crosby), the Buffalo Springfield (Stills), and the Hollies (Nash).

So why add a member, especially one as notoriously eccentric as Neil Young, who had been Stephen Stills's bandmate in the Buffalo Springfield?

"Stephen played both guitar and keyboards on the first record," recalls Crosby. "And when we went to do those

ATLANTIC
1970
David Crosby:
guitar, vocals
Jerry Garcia:
guitar (steel),
slide guitar
Graham Nash:
guitar, keyboards,
vocals
Greg Reeves:
bass, percussion
John Sebastian:
harmonica
Stephen Stills:
bass, guitar, keyboards,
vocals
Dallas Taylor:
drums, percussion
Neil Young:
guitar, harmonica, keyboards, piano, vocals
Produced by
Crosby, Stills, Nash
& Young

songs [live], there were times when he needed to be on the organ, and we needed another guitar player." Of course Young was much more than "another guitar player. Inviting Young was Stills's idea, and neither Crosby nor Nash was sure about it at first.

Crosby remembers Young playing him some songs for the first time: "He just sang me four, five, six songs in a row, and I knew he was one of the best songwriters in the world."

But they were soon convinced by Young's enthusiasm and songwriting ability. Crosby remembers Young playing him some songs for the first time: "He just sang me four, five, six songs in a row, and I knew he was one of the best songwriters in the world."

While *Déjà vu* is one of CSNY's greatest moments, as individuals or as a collective, the recording of the album isn't an entirely great memory for Crosby.

"It was a hard time for me. My girlfriend had just been in a car wreck and got killed. I was completely unable to deal with it. There were times that I was almost useless in the studio 'cause I was so sad. I'd just break down and cry and sit on the floor." Still, *Déjà vu* yielded two of his signature songs: "Almost Cut My Hair" and "Déjà vu." "Almost Cut My Hair" became a counter-culture anthem, but Crosby doesn't count it among his finest moments. "It was the most juvenile set of lyrics I've ever written, and it's certainly not great poetry, but it has a certain emotional impact, there's no question about that."

The album's title track, however, was a taste of what was to come from Crosby: "It's definitely not the normal song structure. When I sent Graham a tape of it, he couldn't believe it. 'There's no chorus, there's no bridge, what is it?' But he loved it, he encouraged me a lot with it. It set the tone for a lot of my writing from then on."

Contrary to myth, Crosby, Stills, Nash and Young worked together on all of the songs, regardless of the author; that is, except for on one song: "4 + 20," written and performed entirely by Stills. Why did CS & Y leave that one alone? "We just said, 'It's too damn good. We're not touching it,'" recalls Crosby. On other songs, CSNY called in some big-name help. John Sebastian of the Lovin' Spoonful played mouth harp on "Déjà vu," and Jerry Garcia played pedal steel guitar on "Teach Your Children," written by Nash. That song, along with "Our House," another Nash composition, went on to become the album's biggest hits, along with "Woodstock" (written for the band by their friend, Joni Mitchell).

Sadly, the CSNY union was too good to last; there were aborted reunion albums, CSN albums, Crosby/Nash albums, a Stills-Young Band album, and lots of guesting on each other's solo records in the decades to come. CSNY wouldn't release another album until 1988's *American Dream*, which was "followed" by *Looking Forward* in 1999. Many fans lament the fact that David Crosby, Stephen Stills, Graham Nash and Neil Young couldn't get their collective act together to record more often. Indeed, years later, Nash wrote "Wasted on the Way," about that very

> *"It was a hard time for me. My girlfriend had just been in a car wreck and got killed. I was unable to deal with it. There were times that I was almost useless in the studio 'cause I was so sad. I'd just break down and cry and sit on the floor."*

issue. "No question we could have made more music," Crosby allows, but adds, "We were lucky even to finish *Déjà vu*," thanks to the various issues the members were dealing with. But his confidence in the album hasn't waned in the decades since they recorded it: "I think it stands up really well, I think we did an excellent job. I think it was a milestone of an album."

B.I.

Straight Outta Compton

62

With its ominous foreboding message proclaiming "you are now about to witness the strength of the street knowledge" and the subsequent percussive overload that sounds like militant marching feet, NWA's *Straight Outta Compton* evoked a more incendiary atmosphere in its first ten seconds than the entire history of rap music up until that point. As such, it was the catalyst for the next wave of rap—mainly, the gangsta preoccupation that Public Enemy's landmark *It Takes a Nation of Millions to Hold Us Back*, released earlier the same year, had only hinted at. Public Enemy's *raison d'etre* had been self-assertion and power through mobilization. But when one looked at the cover of *Straight Outta Compton* and saw the six angry young men on the cover—one of which was brandishing a handgun—it was obvious that NWA's message wasn't just

PRIORITY
1988
Ice Cube:
MC
Dr. Dre:
producer, MC
Eazy-E:
MC
MC Ren:
MC
Yella:
percussion
The D.O.C.:
MC
Produced by
Dr. Dre and Yella

political. What NWA did was turn rap totally into a street phenomenon whereby the mainstream culture at large found itself succumbing to the tenets of ghetto

Their arrival signaled a whole new era of black consciousness in America, a more militant stance that was a direct response to two terms of Ronald Reagan.

culture in order to keep up. It was the first time such lowbrow intentions had become such an all-encompassing force (although surely both rock 'n' roll and disco had hinted at it).

Despite their blatant bad intentions, the members of NWA—or at least three of them, Dr. Dre, Ice Cube, and Eazy-E— were no mere street thugs. For one thing, Dr. Dre, who's probably the most renowned record producer in the world today, set the precedent for artistic freedom in the rap industry by being the first member of a rap crew to seize the production chair. This all tied in with the gangsta mythology because it represented the same kind of

interwoven fabric of control previously maintained by organizations like the mafia—rap groups suddenly became "posses" and the lyrics grew increasingly violent. Ice Cube, the chief lyricist in NWA, helped introduce not only a whole new streetwise delivery to rap but a new vernacular as well: The name alone, which stood for "Niggers with Attitude," was controversial as was the sudden proliferation of the *n* word as well as the word "bitch" to describe women. Also controversial was the fact that a lot of the songs described, sometimes somewhat gleefully, murder in the first degree.

Unfortunately, this may have been the area where NWA and subsequent gangsta rap groups were the most influential—hip-hop turned into the biggest mass phenomenon in popular culture since the hippie movement in the sixties (punk, which happened in between them, has always remained a mostly fringe preoccupation as far as mainstream tastes go). All of a sudden, gangbangers in baggy pants with baseball caps were everywhere—it seems so commonplace now that it's hard to remember, but looking back, NWA was really the catalyst for all that. Eazy-E, who later died of AIDS, was one of the first to assume the gangsta stereotype, and this influenced hundreds of rappers as well as millions of kids, white and black, across the U.S.

Perhaps that was the real turning point: Whereas Public Enemy could be to some degree disseminated by the white intellectual critics, NWA belonged solely to the kids. The definition of a legitimate "phenomenon" is something that appears unexpectedly as if out of the ether and takes the culture by surprise. This is exactly what NWA did, but they couldn't have done it if the album hadn't thumped with the kind of aural immediacy that made their words all the more menacing. Despite some critics' moral qualms about their message, there was no doubt that NWA were merely evoking their environ-ment—admittedly with some degree of bravado—just as socially conscious artists like James Brown and Marvin Gaye had earlier. Their arrival signaled a whole new era of black consciousness in America, a more militant stance that was a direct response to two terms of Reagan. As the most populous and multiethnic state in America (as well as the state that spawned

With its ominous message and the subsequent percussive over-load, Compton evoked a more incendiary atmosphere in its first ten seconds than the entire history of rap up until that point.

Reagan in the first place), California was about to erupt into a newly polarized cli-mate later epitomized by such events as the Los Angeles riots and the O.J. Simpson trial. Long before that, NWA was already evoking a whole new era of urban reality, the consequences of which are still being felt today.   J . S . H .

Superfly

WEA
1972
Curtis Mayfield:
composer, vocals
Produced by
Curtis Mayfield

Everyone knows Curtis Mayfield, the urban pimp. When mentioning the *Superfly* soundtrack, three tunes come instantly to mind: the lubricated groove of the title track, the slick-yet-gritty cool of "Pusherman," and the pumping, hat-cocked prowl that is "Freddie's Dead." These songs alone, fine though they are and sufficient though they might be for any number of lesser lights, are often mistaken for the whole of Curtis Mayfield's solo career, or the whole of his landmark *Superfly* album, at least. What a pity! Curtis's greatness *begins* there, and—with no disrespect to Isaac Hayes (whose songwriting genius was sufficiently proven before he even launched his solo career, and whose brilliance as an arranger and interpreter is fully displayed on the excellent *Hot Buttered Soul,* among other records)—his original movie music is far more than just "movie music," as cannot really be said for the countless soundtracks to the innumerable *other* "Blaxploitation" films of the period. *Shaft,* Marvin Gaye's *Trouble Man;* these are essentially singles with a bunch of varying-quality filler tacked on. *Superfly* is an album proper (shoot, some of Gaye's "real" albums of the period don't match it for quality), and as such, deserves more respect than it gets. "Little Child, Running Wild"—demoed some years previous for Curtis's debut *Curtis* LP—is a sweet-voiced ghetto lament; "No Thing on Me" is typically gorgeous Curtis, slinky and beautiful and tight. The pensive instrumentals, "Think" and "Junkie Chase," are in fact among the album's highlights, not keyboard-doodles with gratuitous *wikka-wikka* guitars but actual songs, gospel-toned soul as deep as anything—in fact, everything—Mayfield recorded with the Impressions and on his first few solo albums.

Mayfield's career was a indeed a rich and fertile one, from those early sides with the Impressions (which influenced, perhaps more than any other American musician, a whole run of

Indeed, more than any single figure other than Bob Dylan, Mayfield might have been responsible for lifting pop music away from its earliest girls-and-Cadillacs obsession.

exquisite Jamaican rocksteady and ska singles) to the socially conscious numbers he waxed on his own Curtom label (and with which the tunes on *Superfly* were of a piece, lest anyone think he was *celebrating* the elephant-lapeled ghetto kingpins that Hollywood was so quick to glamorize.) Indeed, more than any single figure other than Bob Dylan, Mayfield might have been responsible for lifting pop music away from its earliest girls-and-Cadillacs obsession. He brought the church to the people and the people to the church, so to speak. When listening to *Superfly*, feel free to bob your neck and think mack-daddy thoughts, to enjoy the stately yet stanky pimp-liness of it all (a whole generation of hip-hop players, after all, owe their very livelihoods to this man, also, as much as to James Brown), but remember this is the real deal. It runs oh so much deeper than that. M.S.

64

Bitches Brew

Few albums elicited as much controversy upon their release as *Bitches Brew*. Of course for Miles, who had thrown his audience a curveball on a couple of occasions, this kind of notoriety was nothing new. But what proved enduring about *Bitches Brew* was that it didn't just represent another brief foray for its creator—indeed, the electric preoccupation was a lasting phase that would continue throughout the remainder of Davis's career.

At the time, Miles's embrace of electric elements embittered purists, but it was typical of Davis's whole modus operandi as a jazz provocateur and changeling. At the same time, it won him a whole new audience and made him a superstar in the multidimensional and ever-widening rock scene. He became a fixture at legendary rock auditoriums like the Fillmore. He also forged a new approach to electric jazz that was directly responsible for the birth of fusion. Far from being just an interesting experiment, *Bitches Brew* qualifies as one of those albums responsible for spawning a whole new genre of music.

One can hear this music unfurl in the six tracks that make up this double album: the big-band-on-acid maelstrom of "Pharoah's Dance"; the cross-pollinating rhythms of "John McLaughlin"; the New Orleans-by-way-of-Venus bleating of "Miles Runs Down the Voodoo"; the urban funk sprawl of "Spanish Key"; the tranquil glaze of Shorter's "Sanctuary"; and the sinewy funk of "Bitches Brew" itself.

In the end, perhaps what was most impressive about *Bitches Brew* was that it achieved what all such similar high-reaching musical experiments aim to do, which is that it sounded like nothing else ever recorded before. Meanwhile, the influence of *Bitches Brew* still resonates in the percolating rhythms and embryonic textures of fusionaires— as well as math-rockers—everywhere.   J.S.H.

COLUMBIA
1970
Miles Davis:
trumpet
Wayne Shorter:
soprano saxophone
Bennie Maupin:
bass clarinet
Herbie Hancock, Joe Zawinul, Chick Corea, Larry Young:
electric piano
John McLaughlin:
guitar
Dave Holland, Ron Carter, Harvey Brooks:
electric bass
Billy Cobham, Jack DeJohnette:
drums
Airto Moreira, Don Alias, Jim Riley:
percussion
Produced by
Teo Macero

Achtung Baby

ISLAND
1991
Bono:
vocals, guitar
The Edge:
guitar, keyboards,
vocals
Adam Clayton:
bass
Larry Mullen Jr.:
drums, percussion
Produced by
Daniel Lanois with
Brian Eno

It was the last LP. Everything after would be digital. It was the fall of 1991. A friend of mine, a DJ for the Smith College radio station, dropped by on a warm September afternoon with a promotional copy of the new U2 album on vinyl, Anton Corbijn's saturated shots were laid out like exotic stamps on the front and back cover, including the uncensored image of Adam's fig, permanently censored on the CD release. I took the album nonchalantly, promising to check it out and get it back to her. I'd grown weary of U2 during the phenomenal suc-

cess of *The Joshua Tree* and didn't have high expectations for *Achtung*, especially given the mixed results of *Rattle and Hum*.

But my housemate was a freak for the band, bought each album faithfully on the day of release, picked up all the import singles, and forgave Bono his messiah complex. The idea that he'd be psyched, coupled with the fact that we were going to be among the first to check out this record, was cause enough for celebration. We washed down a cocktail of Nyquil and chloraseptic, dropped the needle on the vinyl, lay down on

Achtung Baby

the floor of my bedroom, and got sucked into the brand-new sound of rock and roll.

Gone were the drenched-in-delay arpeggios, gospel anthems, and Christian-existentialist rhetoric, the hallmarks of U2 in the eighties. Here were sick, apocalyptic riffs, industrial drumbeats and world-weary lyrics: "And I'd join the movement / If there was one I could believe in / Yeah I'd break bread and wine / If there was a church I could receive in." For a band that had spent ten years conquering the world, this was hardly a celebration of their hard-fought success. This was a testament to turmoil manifesting itself in songs so personal, so surprisingly intimate, that my first thought was that it was a divorce album. The undercurrent of bitterness, confusion, and search for reconciliation had me convinced Bono had split from his wife. On the contrary.

Turns out there was another divorce in the works: the band itself. Suffering from a lack of direction at the outset of the recordings, U2 describe the early *Achtung* sessions as the most

Gone were the hallmarks of U2 in the '80s. Here were sick apocalyptic riffs, industrial drumbeats and world-weary lyrics.

difficult in their career, a time when they genuinely considered packing it in. Brian Eno was called in partway through to add some levity to the proceedings, and to try to make sense out of the many hours of tape that had been amassed. What easily could have been U2's *Let It Be* turned out to be a shimmering masterpiece. It's a meditation on life at the crossroads, love after the honeymoon, spirituality after blind faith has burned out. All of this playing itself out over loose grooves, exotic rhythms, experimental soundscapes, and lush arrangements, music that is huge when it needs to be, and spare when it has to be.

In the summation song, "Love is blindness / I don't want to see / Won't you wrap the night / Around me," the Edge plucks out a minimalist, haunting solo, teasing tones out of a single note without the slightest hint of melodrama. It wasn't just the Derrida in our heads, this was pure deconstructionism. But with *Achtung Baby*, U2 built the bridge between the analogue past and the digital future.   J.H.

Kind of Blue

66

Here we have an icy-cool icon fronting a band of inspired players recording improvisations in (most cases) a single take in just two days. Is it rock 'n' roll? Of course not. Is it one of the greatest albums ever? Definitely.

Miles Davis played music professionally for more than fifty years, and gradually enveloped himself in a mystique so dark and alluring that his efforts were often the only jazz records in rock fans' collections. Lucky then that he lived up to the hype, maintaining a stringent standard of musical integrity and inventiveness until his death in 1991. *Kind of Blue*, remains a high-water mark.

> **COLUMBIA**
> 1959
> **Miles Davis:**
> trumpet and leader
> **Julian Adderly:**
> alto saxophone
> **John Coltrane:**
> tenor saxophone
> **Wyn Kelly:**
> piano
> **Bill Evans:**
> piano
> **Paul Chambers:**
> bass
> **James Cobb:**
> drums
> **Produced by**
> Teo Macero

This record contains no guitars and no vocals, but its creation and sound would predate the experimentation of rock in the decade to come. The liner notes speak of scales and modes, measures, and circular forms, but it essentially boils down to this: on *Kind of Blue*, Miles Davis assembled a killer jazz band and ordered them to play on themes rather than songs. Think of bringing together Elvis's band in the same year, and giving them simple scales and note clusters on which to jam, rather than chord sheets and lyrics, and you begin to get the picture.

The sound is open and mellow here, but always percolating beneath the surface. "So What" runs two notes up and down while opening up the gates for precise, cutting solos. "All Blues" sounds like music floating in the air, in no hurry, before gently reaching a soft conclusion like a welcoming insight. The songs here are indeed like circles, albeit ones that wander before closing. It helps that the personnel on the record are astounding, with Julian "Cannonball" Adderley and John Coltrane leading what amounts to an embarrassment of riches.

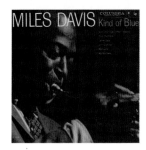

Writing about music, it is said, is like dancing about architecture. Documenting the sound of this astounding record is like describing an hour spent in lively contemplation. Suffice to say that *Kind of Blue* never sounds the same way twice, and always sounds incredibly cool. And that's why rockers always want to claim the cantankerous old iconoclast as one of their own.   Q.S.

Beggars Banquet

1968 was a year of decisions for the Rolling Stones. The psychedelic preoccupation that had revolutionized rock in the wake of the Beatles' *Sgt. Pepper* had never really suited their needs. Their one attempt at it, *Their Satanic Majesties Request* was admittedly a failure. Not surprisingly, the Stones sought to eradicate any whiff of lingering paisley foolishness with a sledgehammer riff in the form of "Jumpin' Jack Flash," their hardest slab of Chuck Berry-inspired rock in two years. They followed that with "Street Fighting Man," another basic rock riff that voiced its primal intentions clearly.

The "back to the roots revival" that was occurring as a backlash to psychedelia wasn't exclusive to the Stones—the Beatles were also getting back to basics with songs like "Lady Madonna" and "Revolution" and albums like *The White Album*, which featured sparse arrangements and more personal songwriting. Always willing to play "yin" to the Beatles's "yang," the Stones released *Beggars Banquet* around the same time in a similarly unadorned sleeve (actually, a result of the Stones's original cover concept—which featured a toilet—

getting banned) and not surprisingly, it was a similarly rustic opus.

Beggars Banquet represented a turning point for the group in more ways than one. For one thing, it would be the last album recorded with guitarist Brian Jones, who'd increasingly become a liability to the group due to his volatile emotional makeup, not to mention his chronic struggles with the law, which had handicapped the group by preventing them from touring America. Although he's still officially listed as a member on *Beggars*, his contributions are reputedly minimal (a fact evidenced by Jean-Luc Godard's film *Sympathy for the Devil*, which shows the Stones recording that opus over and over with Jones apparently unmiked). It was also the first album recorded with producer Jimmy Miller, who'd guide the Stones through what many consider their most fruitful period where they'd record, in succession, four of the greatest rock 'n' roll albums of all time: *Beggars Banquet, Let It Bleed, Sticky Fingers,* and *Exile on Main Street.* In this sense,

---

LONDON RECORDS
1968
Mick Jagger:
vocals, maracas, harmonica
Keith Richards, Brian Jones:
guitars
Bill Wyman:
bass
Charlie Watts:
drums
Nicky Hopkins:
piano
Rocky Dijon:
percussion
Produced by
Jimmy Miller

Beggars can be seen as the catalyst for this renewed period of vigor for the group.

Truth be told, there aren't many albums as complete in their focused excellence as *Beggars Banquet.* The absolute antithesis of trippy meandering, this album rests solely on the vocal and instrumental prowess of its purveyors—given its sparse texture, there is little to cover up on *Beggars Banquet.* Blues ("Prodigal Son," "Parachute Woman") mixes with country ("Dear Doctor") mixes with Dylanesque mumbo-jumbo ("Jig Saw Puzzle") mixes with hard rock ("Stray Cat Blues"). Perhaps most striking is the centerpiece of the album, the opening cut, "Sympathy for the Devil," where Mick finally admits what many had been suspecting all along—that the undercurrent of evil was alive and well in the personages of the Rolling Stones. In this sense, *Beggars Banquet* raised the group's mantle to *mythic*—if not ultimately damning—proportions. This album was a triumph no matter how you look at it.   J . S . H .

Darkness on the Edge of Town

For anyone who might have thought Bruce Springsteen couldn't sustain the creative arc and evolutionary path attained on his breakthrough album, *Born to Run, Darkness on the Edge of Town* proved them soundly wrong. With this astounding album, the New Jersey native took his bar-band boogie from the boardwalk to sold-out shows across the States and let everyone know that he would forever be "The Boss."

With a title that hints at the invisible corners in life that some can't see into and others choose not to see at all, *Darkness*'s lyrics represent a streetwise poeticism that is lofty without being highbrow and straightforward without being simplistic. From the badlands to the Promised Land with the wastelands and the heartland in between, Springsteen travels across the American dream as his cast of outsiders, dreamers, and quiet failures yearn for redemption, wisdom, and escape. On "Prove It All Night" he sings "Everybody's got a hunger, a hunger they can't resist / There's so much that you want, you deserve much more than this," epitomizing that basic sense of hope that his songwriting of this period captured so eloquently. You got the sense when you listened to Springsteen that he wanted the same things as his tortured characters. So, when he sang "For all the shut down strangers and hot rod angels rumbling through this promised land / Tonight my baby and me, we're gonna ride to the sea" in "Racing in the Street," you knew that he too was gonna drive to the sea if it was the last thing he did. And you loved him for it.

Darkness on the Edge of Town helped cement Springsteen's image as the classic American working-class hero and made identification with his work as natural as an appreciation for apple pie, Norman Rockwell paintings, or a '69 Chevy with a 396. The great irony is that Springsteen was a social commentator, oftentimes quite a brutal one, rather than a flag-waving nationalist. Many fans missed this, a paradox that would be further underscored years later with the release of the song "Born in the U.S.A.," which soundly renounces Vietnam-era politics and their subsequent fallout, but was nonetheless seen as the

COLUMBIA
1978
Bruce Springsteen:
lead guitar, vocals, harmonica
Clarence Clemons:
percussion, saxophone, vocals
Roy Bittan:
piano, keyboards
Danny Federici:
organ, keyboards, vocals
Garry Tallent:
bass
Steven Van Zandt:
guitar, vocals
Max Weinberg:
drums
Produced by
Jon Landau

quintessential American theme song. His songs also invoked religious themes that wavered between blind belief and a deeply evocative questioning. No song on the set is more indicative of that than "Adam Raised a Cain," when Springsteen parallels the endless conflict between father and son with two of the good book's greatest fallen souls; "You're born into this life paying / For the sins of somebody else's past."

Kicking up a notch the wall-of-sound aesthetic he had so successfully employed on his previous LP, *Darkness on the Edge of Town* takes out all the exuberance and joy from the mix and leaves the listener to contemplate the music's somber underbelly. This set of material ranks as one of the great examples of American songwriting and helped place Bruce in the pantheon alongside the likes of Bob Dylan and Johnny Cash. And that is where he remains decades later, still standing as one of the most vital and influential rock 'n' roll artists of all time. N.M.

Raw Power

My father gave me a Stooges record when I was ten years old. It was, I'm sure, an accident: Someone in his office had given it to him and he passed it along, unthinking, to me. I took one look at the four leather-jacketed malcontents glaring malignantly from the album's cover and buried it in the back of my closet. I believe I was actually (and justly) afraid of it. Mostly, however, I was embarrassed by my father's misguided efforts to grab my already-drifting attention. If I had actually *played* the record that day, however, he certainly would have had it.

A few years later, when I felt closer in spirit if not in fact to those hoodlums on the album cover, I did. No box of explosives could have been more impressive, no pornography more instructive. And while I retain a wide place in my heart for the loutish, *dunt-dunt-dunt* anthems, the three-chord odes to boredom that comprise that first Stooges album, and for the insane free-jazz squall of their second, *Funhouse* (which sounds like nothing so much as a gang of autistic factory workers mauling the James Brown songbook), it is their third, *Raw Power,* which stands as the band's high-water mark. Nothing, not even the previous two, could have prepared me for my first encounter with *that* record: newbie James Williamson's paint-peeling guitar, pure treble, blasting through my speakers with Iggy's apeshit screaming on "Search and Destroy."

The taut, acoustic "Gimme Danger," which dissolves three-quarters of the way through into washes of feedback that are almost, somehow, poignant. If I'd never heard music like this before it's because it didn't exist, and still doesn't, really, apart from this album.

Williamson is brilliant throughout, as on the flame-fingered "Shake Appeal" (lurid even by this band's formidable standard), the shivering riffage of "Penetration" (ditto).

But this is Iggy's record, of course: On "Your Pretty Face Is Going to Hell," he opens up and delivers a vocal so tremorous, so crusted with gravel and dirt, it sounds like he's singing from the center of the earth. Elsewhere, as on the punishing title track, he delivers no more—and

ELEKTRA
1973
Iggy Pop:
vocals
Ron Asheton:
bass, guitar, vocals
Scott Asheton:
drums
James Williamson:
guitar, vocals
Produced by
Iggy Pop

no less—than that title implies. But any number of singers, before and since (especially since), can claim to deliver "Raw Power." None but Iggy have done so with such a soulful control, such an electrical, almost an elegant vitality. He invents and inhabits these songs, so that even the most unremarkable among them (the lurching, bluesy "I Need Somebody," for instance) becomes thrilling.

It's alarming, if not entirely surprising, to consider that the band's record label, Elektra, was reluctant to release the album at the time; only David Bowie's intelligent, if emasculating, remix of the chaotic master tapes persuaded them.

Years later, Pop remixed it again, and it still sounds like shit. Grimy, trebly, and murky all at once. This, of course, is the album's glory: a sound that cannot, really, be captured; that refuses, somehow, to stand and give a coherent account of itself. All the best rock 'n' roll is like this, however, and it's difficult to imagine it ever gets better than *Raw Power*.   M . S .

Call Me

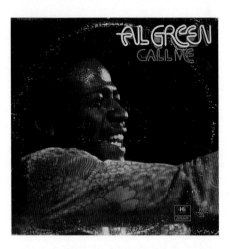

Al Green is dangerous. While this statement isn't one of the sulty imperatives Green used to title his string of mind-bending, loin-firing opuses of the mid-seventies *(Is Love, Is Blues, Gets Next To You!)*, it is nonetheless true. Hearing Al Green as a baffled, sexually frustrated adolescent—or, for that matter, as an adult traversing the same condition—I could believe that somewhere, someone, namely Green, was having the sex I'd always dreamed of: a soul-quaking, window-rattling, sheet-soaking experience for which no adequate descriptive exists. Except, of course, for the albums, which amount to a kind of antipornography; they left one, or left me at least, feeling *clean* and sated, hungry all over again before the cycle was even complete. To give these records to a teenage boy would be like feeding a dreamy girl romance novels, or lending a nun a feather-duster and some baby oil. Corrupting, in other words, and hurtful even in a best-case scenario. But revisiting *Call Me*, the fifth and best of these albums (although *Livin' for You* and the remarkable *Belle Album* come close) as an adult, it's amazing just how nourishing Green's music can be. Produced, brilliantly, by Willie Mitchell, and executed with telepathic exactitude by a band that included the Hodges Brothers, Leroy, Charles and "Teenie" on bass, organ, and guitar, respectively, the music is pillowy, without any of the drippy, lubricious excesses that mar even some of the finest records of Green's contemporaries: Mssrs. Gaye, White, Hayes, etc. Backing vocals are spare; strings are occasional, pushed back in the mix. A churchy grit prevails, the better to let Al—now the Right Reverend Green, thank you very much—take center stage.

With a vocal style so convicted, so urgent on the one hand, so teasing on the other, Green moans, whispers, shivers, hollers, begs . . . in short, he testifies, so intimately you can almost believe—here, the paradox—he is talking to himself. On the glorious "Your Love Is Like the Morning Sun," on stunning covers of Hank Williams ("I'm So Lonesome I Could Cry") and Willie Nelson ("Funny How Time Slips Away"), Green could bend the

CAPITOL
1973
Al Green:
vocals
Mabon "Teenie" Hodges:
guitar
Leroy Hodges:
bass
Charles Hodges:
organ, piano
Archie Turner:
piano
Howard Grimes, Al Jackson Jr.:
drums
The Memphis Strings:
strings
Jack Hale, Wayne Jackson, Andrew Love, James Mitchell:
horns
Charles Chalmers, Donna Rhodes, Sandra Rhodes:
background vocals
Produced by
Willie Mitchell

stars to pity. On "Stand Up" and the utterly silken title song, he sounds ready to hang himself up there among them, while the lean and greasy "Here I Am (Come and Take Me)" roots the album down in the Memphis mud, more corporeal than ever. And on the album's mighty centerpiece, "Jesus Is Waiting," Green sinks to his knees—both figuratively and, from the sound of it, literally—to beg forgiveness, his pleas so quivering you can practically hear the panties landing on stage. This, of course, is the crux of the matter. The more heated, the more erotic, the more explicit the record becomes, the more divine, and vice versa. Green restores the sex to religion, and the sanctity to the bedroom, always a dangerous proposition. On later albums, notably *Belle Album*, he would reverse the proportions, and place what amounted to full-blown obscene phone calls to God. Here, he drags the Lord down to the couch and licks his ear. Listen, and be duly moved. M.S.

Physical Graffiti

By 1975, Led Zeppelin had reached their absolute zenith. Indeed it was the day and age of the utmost rock grandiosity, and Zeppelin were at the pinnacle of the rock spectrum in all terms of excess as well as success. Having come off an incredibly successful, lengthy North American tour, which was as legendary for its stunning theatrics as it was for the band's lavish and decadent touring lifestyle, Zeppelin resided at the very top of the hard-rock heap and in many ways had fully usurped the titans of the previous decade: the Beatles, the Rolling Stones, and Bob Dylan (a fact the critics were never quite willing to grant them). But the one thing Zeppelin to this point had never done was release a double album. They'd toyed with folk and classical embellishments, blues affectations, and progressive airs, not to mention the most molten of heavy-metal; on *Physical Graffiti* they made use of all these idioms in a way that even their longtime detractors had to admit showed a newfound "maturity" for this

ATLANTIC RECORDS
1975
Robert Plant:
vocals
Jimmy Page:
guitars
John Paul Jones:
bass, keyboards
John Bonham:
drums
Produced by
Jimmy Page

band of rogues. But what very few people realized at the time was that *Physical Graffiti* was more or less a compilation.

Like other patchwork LPs from the same era, such as Miles Davis's *Get Up with It* or Dylan's *The Basement Tapes*, it wasn't so much a thematic entity as it was a tossed-

By 1975, Zeppelin had reached their absolute zenith. They were at the pinnacle of the rock spectrum in all terms of excess as well as success.

together assemblage of odds and ends left over from a finite period of recording activity. Therefore it's very hard to say exactly what Physical *Graffiti* "represents"—instead it's more accurate to see it almost as a microcosm of all the various idioms the band was working on at the time (perhaps, in some cases, to less-than-serious effect). But while *Physical Graffiti* is hardly seamless, it never sounds thrown together. In fact, like the Rolling Stones's *Exile on Main Street*, the expanse of available tracks in many ways

highlights the growth of the band itself during those pivotal years of the early seventies. The fact that this LP was cobbled together probably because Jimmy Page was tired after the overwhelming tour in 1973 hardly matters. Far from an afterthought, *Physical Graffiti* is a double album that gets better with age.

A great deal of the material here was recorded during the sessions for the previous LP, 1973's *Houses of the Holy*. An odd distinction of *Physical Graffiti* is that it in fact houses what would've been the title cut from that LP, if Page had chosen to include it. As it turns out, "Houses of the Holy" works brilliantly here and sets the precedent for the LP's midtempo stomp. One thing that's apparent all over the aptly named *Physical Graffiti* is the awesome power of drummer John Bonham, whose center-heavy sound set the groove for the whole band. Other songs, like "The Rover," "Night Flight," and "Sick Again," epitomize the staggering power of Zeppelin in this era, at a time when they were pretty much riding the world with one big erection. "Boogie with Stu," a tossed-off tribute to erstwhile Rolling Stones keyboardist Ian Stewart that dates back to 1971, is a bombastic nod to Zeppelin's rock 'n' roll roots complete with one of Robert Plant's most absurd falsettos and some Jerry Lee Lewis–style piano playing from Stewart himself (who sits in, as does Ritchie Valens's widow).

Of the tracks that were recorded somewhat nearer to the LP's release, two in particular stand out: "Trampled Underfoot," the only single released from *Physical Graffiti*, is absolutely Zeppelin at their best—a sexual innuendo, disguised as an automobile metaphor, backed up by absolutely pile-driving force by the whole band. This song belongs to John Paul Jones, whose funky organ playing, reminiscent of another Stones fave, Billy Preston, makes the track absolutely writhe with licentious intent, bursting into an orgasmic conclusion that has Plant once again yelping like a eunuch coyote. Bonham is absolutely thunderous on this track, as is the whole band. Zeppelin didn't always live up to their pretensions of being the

absolute rock gods, but on this track they evoke a power that is truly mystical.

And speaking of mystical, *Physical Graffiti* also contains what may be, after "Stairway to Heaven," the band's most legendary opus, the 8:31 "Kashmir," the last track recorded for the LP in 1974 and one

> *Songs like "The Rover," and "Sick Again," epitomize the power of Zeppelin at a time when they were riding the world with one big erection.*

reflecting Robert Plant's continued fascination with Eastern mysticism. Not surprisingly, Zep's take on the whole thing is somewhat of a colonialist stance, but what else would you expect from these English lords? Although Zeppelin themselves would probably feel more at home in a castle than in the tenement slums that adorn the LP sleeve, *Physical Graffiti* is about as down to earth as they ever got, and as a double dose of their feudal bombast, it's a surprisingly consistent affair.   J.S.H.

Electric Ladyland

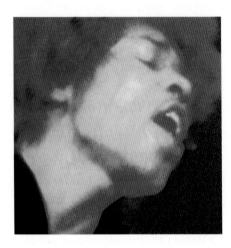

It's tough business, choosing from among the few albums Hendrix recorded during his ridiculously brief tenure as a recording act. But you won't go wrong with the one he named after his studio—for in it is the sound of rock's greatest artist relaxing, stretching out, and letting his genius take him where it would.

It is no exaggeration to say that the vast majority of tracks on *Electric Ladyland* are of such innovative quality and soulful transcendence that one could wear out the CD "replay" button and spend entire evenings letting single songs unfold

hidden dimensions through repeated listening. First there are the tracks that have entered the classic-rock canon: the bristling, uncharacteristically uptight "Crosstown Traffic," and the magnanimous stoned invitation of "Have You Ever Been (to Electric Ladyland)"—Hendrix was always inviting the listener to join him in his sonic world. Soon follows the mind-grenade of "Voodoo Child (Slight Return), and the apocalyptic roar of "All Along the Watchtower" (on which Hendrix managed the difficult feat of wresting away total possession of a Bob Dylan composition). On the strength of these tunes alone could a case be made for Hendrix's immortal greatness.

This was originally a two-LP set, though, and it's in the generous sprawl of *Electric Ladyland* that the magnitude of Hendrix's gifts are revealed. The elephantine blues of the first "Voodoo Child" (there are two on the disk) captures the electricity of Hendrix improvising in the studio; the shimmering "Burning of the Midnight Lamp" snakes through the ears with layers of distortion; and the lengthy freakout of what was the original album's Side C see Hendrix in the full flower of uninhibited, self-indulgent exploration. What would have been stoned meandering from another artist is genius from Hendrix, and the listener wishes the tunes could have gone on forever.

At times on *Electric Ladyland*, it seems as though they might, for the record is an embarrassment of riches. There are sixteen cuts here, and each could be seen to explore another facet of Hendrix's restless artistry: trips through blues, pop, sonic abstraction, and the invention of that

> **MCA RECORDS**
> 1968
> **Jimi Hendrix:**
> vocals, guitar
> **Noel Redding:**
> bass
> **Mitch Mitchell:**
> drums
> **With Mike Finnigan, Freddie Smith, Larry Faucette, Buddy Miles, Chris Wood, Stevie Winwood, Jack Cassidy, and Al Kooper**
>
> **Produced and directed by**
> Jimi Hendrix

elusive thing called "rock music" are all on the agenda. What binds it all together is that other elusive thing: psychedelia, and not just of the paisley-shirt and granny-glasses variety. At its best, the psychedelic art of the sixties sought to break down barriers of all kinds: between genres, between sounds, between the pre-synesthetic isolation of the senses, and between the individual and the collective whole of reality. *Electric Ladyland*, in this sense, is one of the most psychedelic works of art ever created. The songs on this disk break down barriers both musical and lyrical, but perhaps most important is the sound of Hendrix yearning to break down the most daunting barrier of all: that between him and his audience, the listener. This is the sound of Hendrix spreading out, and trying to record the sounds in his mind—because, by doing so, he would have broken down any impediment between himself and the grand, orgiastic totality that his music suggested.

It's that heavy. If only Jimi had had more time.   Q.S.

Grace

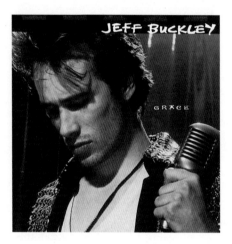

When you mention the name Jeff Buckley, you can tell right away if someone is a fan. A sparkle appears in the eye, the voice gets a little lower, and a look of sadness comes over the face. He's affected them, got into their soul. They own *Grace*.

Like most of us that didn't have their hand on the pulse of the New York music scene, the first time I heard Jeff was on MTV (of all places) when *120 Minutes* played "Last Goodbye." What were these lyrics I was hearing? "This is our last goodbye / I hate to feel the love between us die / But it's over / Just hear this and then I'll go / You

gave me more to live for / More than you'll ever know." I was hooked. To whom was this man singing these heartfelt words? Off to the music store I went to buy what would become one of the most precious pieces of music in my CD collection.

I had no idea what I was getting into. The moment the CD began, a chill ran through my body as I heard his voice signaling the start of "Mojo Pin." I needed to stop breathing just to hear "Hallelujah" in complete silence. He knew everything that I was thinking when he sang "Lover You Should Have Come Over," and it's impossible not to be affected by the raw aggression put forth in "Eternal Life." I was taken on an emotional ride through love and longing, moving through the poetic lyrics flowing out from deep within his soul. Combine that with the purest outpouring of music any artist could offer and you have a work of art.

I wasn't the only one who came to know this album. Jeff Buckley's name would start to pop up in social circles as friends told one another what albums they needed to add to their collection. One would start to hear him on the radio, see him sporadically on TV. He was this little secret that the music community was just beginning to share with the rest of the world. As I would find out later, he came to influence more musicians with one album than most artists do with a lifetime of work.

Because of *Grace*, I started to collect anything I could get my hands on from Jeff, from the European and Australian singles put out from *Grace* to the *Live at Sin-é* EP, the first major-

COLUMBIA
1994
Jeff Buckley:
voice, guitars, harmonica, organ, dulcimer, tabla
Mick Grondahl:
bass
Matt Johnson:
drums, percussion, vibes
Michael Tighe:
guitar
Gary Lucas:
guitar
Loris Holland:
organ
Misha Masud:
tabla
Produced by
Andy Wallace and Steven Berkowitz

label recording of Jeff that showcased his incredible talent of playing live and entrancing an audience. Sadly, the one thing I never got to do was see him live. I just figured I'd see him next time. Little did I know.

In May of 1997, just out of college and getting started in my career as a music journalist, I was working for MTVRadio in New York City when I "found" the news. In the press release that had come over the fax that day was the horrible truth—Jeff Buckley was missing, assumed drowned in the Mississippi River. I was shaken. I had never known the man, but he touched my soul through *Grace*. A week later, the news was confirmed—Jeff was found dead in the river. The artist was gone from this earth and with him went the music we would never get to hear.

Yes, there have been those posthumous releases, songs that Jeff worked on during his lifetime. I'll gladly collect them all, but it's not the same. *Grace* is like a gift from the heavens. I guess they wanted their angel back. H.S.

Paul's Boutique

Paul's Boutique was significant because the Beasties made a record and didn't care what anybody thought. They wanted to make the antithesis to *License to Ill*. But let us not forget the impact of *License to Ill* by the Beasties collective with Rick Rubin, in saying this is the record that we have to make the impact. The fact that *License to Ill* and *Paul's Boutique* were so drastically different was a template that I used in my career.

—CHUCK D

A friend of mine pinned me down and made me listen. This was in the late eighties, when rap as I understood it (or frankly, failed to understand it) consisted of men hollering boastful rhymes over booming beats; fine as things went, on a car radio or at a party, but not really, y'know, rewarding when it came to closer listening. Ridiculous as this admission sounds with the benefit of hindsight (where would we be, without twenty years of glorious and not-so-glorious hip-hop? Is there any sound fresher, in every sense of the word, than those first, Sugarhill twelve-inches?), at the time it made sense. I couldn't have been less interested in a sophomore effort by the Beastie Boys, whose first album seemed little more than boosted Zeppelin-riffs complemented with a cute-the-first-few-times video. How was I to know *Paul's Boutique* would rearrange my thoughts as thoroughly as *Sgt. Pepper's* had, reportedly, for listeners twenty years before? But the dusted-soul organ of "To All the Girls" faded in over the headphones (my friend was forcing me to pay full homage), then exploded into the spastic disco whooping of "Shake Your Rump," and I realized, immediately, I'd been wrong. The songs were crammed full, impossibly juiced with things I recognized, and—more tantalizingly—things I didn't. There were the shower-strings from *Psycho* rubbing up with Curtis Mayfield's "Superfly" riff ("Egg Man"); there were multilayered Beatles samples ("The Sound of Science,"); there were fleeting interjections from everyone from Bob Marley to Joey Ramone. There were far more obscure steals from Sly Stone (the irresistible "Shadrach"), rare-groove riffs slowed down to half-speed and plastered over with stoner-rock guitars and goofy, whispered admonitions ("Take PCP!") The record was an encyclopedia, a thesis; something (or many things, actually) borrowed transfigured into something utterly new.

And while a good deal if not all of the credit for the album's *sound* must go to its visionary producers, the Dust Brothers, it's the album's spirit, its magnificent wit and supersaturated *jeu d'esprit,* that make it more than an amusing patchwork of past-dated influences. Ad-

CAPITOL
1989
MCA, Ad-Rock, Mike D
Produced by
the Beastie Boys,
the Dust Brothers

Rock's adenoidal bragging; MCA's bodega Buddhism; Mike D's lipstick-killer brilliance. The three MCs in question *own* this album, slinging deliriously ridiculous rhymes ("Geraldo Rivera" with "pasta primavera," for instance) so rapidly it's as if the mic grip's on fire. Impossible to resist the chest-bump swagger of "What Goes Around" or the full-on goofery of "Hey Ladies," for example. By the time the album gets around to the epic collage of "B-Boy Bouillabaisse"— which cuts up funk beats and genius rhymes so furiously it's like twelve televisions (all vintage cop-shows and seventies porn, of course) going at once—one's head is spinning, or rather, spun. I owe to this record a taste for any number of other hip-hop masterpieces— without it, a Tribe Called Quest's *The Low End Theory* or De La Soul's *3 Feet High and Rising* might've been beyond me—but even after its influences, and its influence, have been parsed, *Paul's Boutique* remains a brilliant entity unto itself, as word-drunk as vintage Dylan and as sonically inventive as rock albums come.   M.S.

Let It Be

The early eighties saw pop reign with an iron heel. It was the age of the hyper-produced megahit. For young music lovers, it was the equivalent of plodding across a barren desert. Where was our genius, and who was going to take our yearnings and set them to kick-ass music? When was the eighties generation going to come up with something better than synth-pop and microwaved Roxy Music leftovers? The answer came from way up north, in Minnesota, the land of low sun and frozen lakes. That urban hinterland was festering with the antidote to a moment in music distinguished primarily by vapidity—bands that were flying low to the ground and bringing teenage soul back to rock 'n' roll. The greatest of them were the Replacements.

They were snotty and bratty—take their ridiculous hubris in copping a Beatles' album title, for starters. They were famously inebriated. They dressed like they had

TWIN/TONE
1984
Paul Westerberg:
guitar,
keyboards, vocals
Bob Stinson:
guitar
Tommy Stinson:
bass
Chris Mars:
drums
Produced by
Paul Westerberg,
Steven Fjelstad,
Peter Jesperson

grabbed the first thing they found from the dusty floor of the Salvation Army. But behind their willful don't-give-a-shit attitude was a band toward whom the yearnings of countless misfits, weirdos, stoners, and losers with hearts of gold would gravi-

Anyone who ever drank four beers on a Saturday night and screamed down a dark alley will immediately understand the blitzed insouciance of "Gary's Got a Boner" and "Tommy Gets His Tonsils Out."

tate. It was the songs of Paul Westerberg, reluctant genius, that locked into the hearts of young people looking for soul and screw-it-all defiance against the homogenized sounds they were being expected to consume. This is, notice, one of the very few LPs on this list that was originally released on an independent label.

No one knows more than Westerberg how much weight was placed on this young band's shoulders. The Replacements were determined to be indie commandos, to cut a drunken swath across the decade,

but the limitations of their goals were constantly undermined by the quality of Westerberg's songwriting. This group of misfits, it turned out, was led by one of the best writers in the history of rock music.

So what, exactly, is going on with *Let It Be?* The new generation of music fans might fear that the Replacements are their older brother's band, a group they're supposed to like but whose moment has passed.

Forget about it, buster. Put on the disc. This thing is great from start to finish.

After a few records of punk craziness and bursts of garage brilliance, the Replacements brought it all together on *Let It Be.* Listening to "Sixteen Blue" or the aching "Androgynous" is enough to melt the heart of any former teenage misfit. Anyone who ever drank four beers on a Saturday night and screamed down a dark alley will immediately understand the blitzed insouciance of "Gary's Got a Boner" and "Tommy Gets His Tonsils Out." And anyone who ever dared expose their heart to a teenage sweetheart—knowing deep down it would never work out—will hear themselves in "I Will Dare" and the frustrated "Answering Machine." For good measure, they resurrected the old KISS tune "Black Diamond"—making it cool as hell at a moment when KISS were at perhaps their lowest ebb.

The Replacements sounded like four savants strangling their instruments one moment, then cajoling them into ragged beauty the next. The late Bob Stinson's guitar was a revelation, its trashy grind rocking with one eyebrow raised, while his kid brother Tommy (only in his teens) thumped away on bass without a proper permission slip. Westerberg himself was blessed with a voice to match his expansive songwriting talent, infusing his tunes with longing, sadness, rage, and a vocal presence that turned each song into a mixed bag of bittersweet loss and triumph. *Let It Be* saw the Replacements begin to transcend mere thrash, with (gasp) piano and a few songs played slow enough for the emotion to seep out from them like tears out of a lonely eye.

They were the little band who could. Everyone who loved them felt like they loved them best. They went on to make more records, some of them very good ones, then imploded. Westerberg embarked

The Replacements sounded like four savants strangling their instruments one moment, then cajoling them into ragged beauty the next. They were the little band who could.

on a solo career while constantly dogged by comparisons to his former self. It is, of course, monumentally unfair to expect the man to make us feel like we did when we first heard *Let It Be*. It's almost as though Westerberg has to take the rap for our growing older. But the unfairness also contains the kindest of compliments—for anyone who crafted a resonant gem such as *Let It Be* deserves nothing less than the total gratitude of anyone who loves rock music. It's no wonder people just can't seem to let go.   Q.S.

76 Young, Gifted and Black

At the time of the release of *Young, Gifted and Black*, Aretha Franklin was in transition. Often referred to as "Lady Soul" in the sixties, the world was now beginning to know her as "The Queen of Soul." She was coming off her 1970 album, the underrated *Spirit in the Dark*, which hadn't sold as well as prior albums. On the other hand, she was gaining confidence as a writer. For *Young, Gifted and Black* she wrote four songs (one third of the album), which went a long way in displaying that she not only possessed great range as a singer, but also as a songwriter. "All the King's Horses" is a heartbreaking tale of a relationship that didn't make it, likely inspired by the end of her marriage with manager Ted White. "Day Dreaming" and "Last Snow in Kokomo" are gorgeous, lilting, dreamy ballads. On the other hand, "Rock Steady" showed that she could still kick out the jams and rock the party better than anyone when she was in the mood to do so.

Ms. Franklin's considerable composing chops didn't curb her enthusiasm for continuing to interpret other people's songs. For the third time, she dipped into the Beatles' songbook for "The Long and Winding Road" (having previously recorded "Let It Be" and "Eleanor Rigby"). She also did a track by the then-new songwriting team of Elton John and Bernie Taupin, "Border Song." Although Elton's version is one of his greatest hits, it seemed as if it was written with Ms. Franklin in mind.

The title track, a version of a song originally written and recorded by Nina Simone, was a powerful statement for Ms. Franklin, who was pictured on the album cover draped in African garments and a regal headdress. But perhaps the most revealing song on the album was "A Brand New Me."

Young, Gifted and Black shows Aretha Franklin as emotionally honest and intimate as she's ever been, relating the pain of a failed relationship, the joy of a new one, her confidence in her songwriting, not to mention her piano playing, abilities, and her pride in being a black woman. Lady Soul was now ready for her crown.

B.I.

ATLANTIC
1972
Aretha Franklin:
vocals, piano, celeste,
electric piano
Various musicians

Produced by
Jerry Wexler,
Tom Dowd,
Arif Mardin

Sweet Baby James

James Taylor's second album, *Sweet Baby James*, put him at the forefront of the singer-songwriter movement. To his fans, his music is like a favorite pair of jeans: warm, familiar, and comfortable. Of course, most people don't know exactly where or how their jeans were made, and it is quite likely that many people who sit on blankets at amphitheaters summer after summer, listening to Taylor croon "Fire and Rain," the album's most famous track, are probably unaware that the song's genesis came in a mental institution.

While in later years, Taylor became known (perhaps unfairly) as the face of polished soft-rock, Taylor's early years weren't so clean-cut. In the late sixties, he battled depression and drug addiction, and checked into clinics twice to deal with these problems. "Fire and Rain" was, in part, about the suicide of a friend he met at one of these clinics. The subtlety in the song wasn't simply to court commercial radio play, it was to deal with the sensitive topic in an appropriate way. Still, despite its maudlin subject matter, it became one of Taylor's biggest hits. The song would go on to become a sort of anthem to those coping with loss.

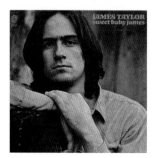

> **WARNER BROS.**
> 1970
> **James Taylor:**
> guitar, vocals
> **Various Musicians**
>
> **Produced by**
> Peter Asher

Of course, *Sweet Baby James* was far from just being a funeral for a friend. The title track was written about his nephew and namesake, although fans would later use the title to refer to James. The album also displays Taylor's sharp sense of wit in the track "Steamroller." Never before and never again in song would Taylor refer to himself as "a napalm bomb—guaranteed to blow your mind." Safe to say that not even Taylor's most ardent fan ever considered him "a churning urn of burning funk." With tongue firmly planted in cheek, Taylor claimed these titles for himself. And with more than just a wink, this blues tribute/parody showed a sense of humor not often associated with Taylor.

However, it is songs like "Fire and Rain" that Taylor is most often associated with, songs that greet you like an old friend, and console you when you need it. And that might be Taylor's appeal: He may not be the idolized rock-star type, but he *is* the guy who can empathize with you when you're down and out because he's been there.

B.I.

78

Axis: Bold as Love

Axis: Bold as Love, the second album by the Jimi Hendrix Experience, represented a giant step forward for the band who were perfecting the concept of the "power trio," a dynamic based solely on the collaborative prowess of its three integrally intertwined members. While *Are You Experienced?* was one of the most auspicious debuts ever, it's tempting to say that the refinement offered by *Axis* was even more rewarding. For one thing,

this was the album where Hendrix really learned how to harness the modern recording studio as an instrument into and of itself—for a guitarist who'd pointed the way toward the infinite possibilities of the guitar and amplification, it was the third prong in the crown that made him one of the most important musical innovators of the era. On *Axis,* tricks with stereo panning and other audiophile traits mix with the band's raw emotion to create one of the true psychedelic masterpieces.

Leading off with spaceship sounds—on the eponymous "EXP"—*Axis* was a bold step toward audio refinement meant to blow minds on the new multichannel speaker systems. Hendrix developed a fruitful working relationship with

engineer Eddie Kramer that resulted in bold sound experiments like the multilayered overdubs in "If Six Was Nine," where Mitchell's almost martial drumming and Redding's railroading bass merged with Hendrix's madly fluctuating guitar leads brilliantly. The emphasis wasn't as much on heaviness this time, as it had been with the group's debut; a lot of the songs were ethereal, like "You Got Me Floatin'," and some were downright sublime in their compassionate embrace of the world around them, like "Little Wing." A lot of this was probably due to LSD, and in lesser hands such mystical notions might have been a disaster. Once again, it's the cohesion of the three players in the band that makes *Axis* a staggering musical experiment.

Check out, for instance, the exuberant bridge of "One Rainy Wish," which explodes into one of Hendrix's most impassioned—and soulful—vocal moments. Or the intensely hot guitar lines that close out the embryonic "Spanish Castle Magic." *Axis* was a multifaceted gem that brought many different exotic styles and musical substances together into a dazzling package. J.S.H.

REPRISE
1968

Jimi Hendrix:
guitars, vocals
Noel Redding:
bass
Mitch Mitchell:
drums

Produced by
Chas Chandler

Ten

EPIC
1991
Eddie Vedder:
vocals
Stone Gossard:
guitars
Mike McCready:
lead guitars
Jeff Ament:
bass
Dave Krusen:
drums
Rick Parashar:
piano, organ, percussion
Walter Gray:
cello
Tim Palmer:
"fire extinguisher,
pepper shaker"
Produced by
Pearl Jam,
Rick Parashar

Certainly one of the most influential albums of the nineties, Pearl Jam's *Ten* spawned countless imitators, helped what was then known as "alternative rock" bumrush the pop music mainstream, and sold millions of records. And, after all was said and done, the band—and especially singer Eddie Vedder—seemed to try to get as far away from it as possible.

But first a little history: Guitarist Stone Gossard and bassist Jeff Ament spent much of the eighties in the Seattle band Green River, a band that combined sixties garage

Certainly one of the most influential albums of the nineties . . . Ten spawned countless imitators and helped "alternative rock" bum-rush the pop music mainstream.

rock with the heaviness of Black Sabbath. The band split up, with vocalist Mark Arm and guitarist Steve Turner going on to form the similarly raw-sounding Mudhoney, while Gossard and Ament moved on to the more polished sounds of Mother Love Bone, led by Freddie Mercury disciple Andrew Wood. MLB were quickly signed to a major label, and seemed to be on the verge of stardom; sadly, Wood died of a drug overdose before their debut album, *Apple*, was released. Once again, Gossard and Ament stuck together and moved forward.

Soon, they formed Pearl Jam with guitarist Mike McCready, drummer Dave Krusen, and singer Eddie Vedder, the latter of whom they met through former Red Hot Chili Peppers (and future Pearl Jam) drummer Jack Irons. *Ten* didn't get too much attention upon its summer 1991 release—it seemed too "mainstream" for "alternative" radio, not "hard" enough for metalheads—but soon the stars would align. After spending a few weeks on the road with the Red Hot Chili Peppers (who were also blowing up in a big way thanks to their *BloodSugarSexMagik* album), they toured on their own, and also played what was arguably one of the best *MTV Unplugged* sets ever. They spent the summer with a highly coveted slot on the Lollapalooza tour, right as *Ten* was picking up serious steam. A conceptual video for "Jeremy" put them all over MTV, and radio constantly played that song as well as several others from the album, including the mosh-friendly "Evenflow," the ballads

"Oceans" and "Black," and especially the mid-tempo anthem "Alive." *Ten* rocketed to number two on the pop albums chart, kept from the top slot by Billy Ray Cyrus's *Some Gave All.* Eddie Vedder was even on the cover of *Time* magazine. Rock radio molded itself in Pearl Jam's image, with playlists dominated by arena-ready rock bands in grunge clothing. And Pearl Jam was getting at least some of the blame.

Nirvana's Kurt Cobain blasted Pearl Jam in *Musician* magazine, calling them "corporate, alternative, and cock rock fusion," later telling *Rolling Stone* "they're jumping on the alternative bandwagon." Less famous indie-rock purists tended to agree. Pearl Jam wouldn't be their whipping boy for long, though: By their next album, 1993's *Vs.,* they'd adopted a grittier sound, and, for the most part, veered clear of *Ten*'s accessibility.

The band would never match the sales of *Ten,* but they had enough fans to allow them a certain amount of freedom not afforded to many bands. They were able to avoid, for the most part, having to do interviews for years, and they only made one music video (which they didn't appear in) post-*Ten.* Their enduring popularity also allowed them freedom to pursue other side projects, and also to release official "live" bootlegs of all the shows on their

Rock radio molded itself in Pearl Jam's image, with playlists dominated by arena-ready rock bands in grunge clothing.

2000 tour. They would also earn the respect of several of their idols: Eddie Vedder has, over the years, shared the stage with the Rolling Stones, the Who, and the surviving members of the Doors; he's recorded with punk-rock icon Mike Watt, world-music titan Nusrat Fateh Ali Khan, and even actress Susan Sarandon. The band has backed up Neil Young and Jim Carroll. All cool achievements, true, but none as staggering as *Ten*—an album with eleven tracks, all of which hold up over a decade later.   B.I.

My Aim Is True

Anger has always been primary among artists' responses to the hypocrisy, perfidy, and treachery of the world—it is the heartbroken soul's means of lashing out and escaping the trap of its own introspective hall of mirrors. Dylan, in his white-hot days of the mid-sixties, spewed venom and romance often in the space of a single dense lyrical line. And, in 1977, along came *My Aim Is True* to harness another great artist's cutting bile into three-minute slices of accusation, condemnation, and lovesick bitterness.

Declan McManus grew up in a musical family,

with a successful bandleader father, and was steeped in British musical tradition—a fact that wouldn't become evident until a few years down the line. For the moment, on his debut album the newly named Elvis Costello (the surname derived from his own family) combined his dense, knowing lyrical slams with taut, guitar-based songs that delivered first a jab, then a hook, then an uppercut to a world that had apparently done him wrong.

Costello's image was disarming, with his over-cuffed jeans, Buddy Holly glasses, and knock-kneed scrawniness. Listeners soon learned that there was nothing guileless or innocent about the new Elvis (and it's hard to imagine today how audacious it was of him to take that name). *My Aim Is True* kicked off with the acerbic "Welcome to the Working Week," and it's worth remembering that Costello was still working his day job when he wrote this collection of songs. The sound is harsh, the vocals spit out of a frothing mouth, but already it was evident that Elvis was more than an angry punk. His chord progressions were deft, often sophisticated, and his lyrics were literate and biting—and often slipped by too fast for American audiences to understand.

"Blame It on Cain" bops along nicely, until the listener realizes that the song is about patsies, losers, and fall guys. "Less Than Zero" is a real foot tapper—and also an acerbic condemnation of British right-wing politics. And "(The Angels Wanna Wear My) Red Shoes," the first song on the flip side in the old pre-CD days, is an excellent slice of sartorial boasting that kicks off with the immortal couplet "Oh, I used to be disgusted, but now I try to be amused." Around

COLUMBIA
1977
Elvis Costello:
drum sticks, guitar, piano, vocals
Various musicians
Produced by
Bill Inglot, Nick Lowe, Andrew Sandoval

this time, Costello famously listed revenge and guilt as his main sources of artistic inspiration. The younger Costello took no poetic solace in bittersweet reflection. He was already an accomplished writer, capable of penning hook after hook, and for the moment he would spare the world none of his scorn.

The exception was "Alison," the one song in which Costello tempered his anger. Addressed to an ex-lover married to another man, "Alison" captured the sadness of the singer watching someone he once loved being crushed by the world. It was as though Costello could sympathize only with a fellow sufferer.

"Alison" was delivered in a shadow of the croon he would later adopt, and foreshadowed the nuance and sophistication to come. Costello spent the next five years releasing a set of musically inventive and lyrically brilliant albums, each of which built on the ambitious blueprint laid out on *My Aim Is True*. He would then assay guitar rock only sporadically, perhaps returning home to variations on his father's traditional band sounds that he heard in his youth.   Q.S.

Otis Blue: Otis Redding Sings Soul

At the center of the album is the voice: Redding had the gift of controlled fury. His singing infused a gritty intensity with boundless emotion.

Those seeking the heart of sixties soul need look no farther. In the course of Otis Redding's brief career as a singer and songwriter, he created some of the most emotive and compelling popular music ever produced. *Otis Blue* plays like a sprawling portfolio of the man's considerable talents.

At the center of the album is the voice: Redding had the gift of controlled fury. His singing infused a gritty intensity with boundless emotion. For all he gave in his performances, he somehow left the impression that there was

81

VOLT
1965

Otis Redding:
vocals

**Wayne Jackson,
Gene "Bowlegs" Miller:**
trumpet

Andrew Love:
tenor sax

Floyd Newman:
baritone sax

**Isaac Hayes,
Booker T. Jones:**
keyboards

Steve Cropper:
guitar

Donald "Duck" Dunn:
bass

Al Jackson Jr.:
drums

Earl Sims:
background vocals

Produced by
Stax Staff

more in reserve, and that you had better keep listening to find out what.

"Respect" (yes, that "Respect," Aretha's masterpiece—he wrote it, too) is pounded out in a little more than two minutes. "Ole Man Trouble" (another Redding composition) is built around a snaking guitar and a vocal of wary sorrow. The delicate arpeggios of "I've Been Loving You Too Long" highlight Redding's stark storytelling. This trio of originals alone comprise a burst of classic writing and singing that raise *Otis Blue* to classic status.

And that's before the covers. Redding is rightly remembered as a master songsmith, but he was also an ace interpreter of other writers' material. *Otis Blue* takes on a series of ambitious covers that might have sounded collectively ridiculous in the hands of a lesser performer. Who else could have tackled Sam Cooke ("Change is Gonna Come," "Shake," and "Wonderful World") the Rolling Stones's

"(I Can't Get No) Satisfaction," The Temptations's "My Girl," B.B. King's "Rock Me Baby" and "You Don't Miss Your Water" on the same LP? Redding was the rare singer with the capacity to make a listener forget the original version of a song he covered—his sinewy take on "Wonderful World" alone achieved the near-impossible task of matching Sam Cooke. And, in the process, Redding metaphorically repaid a debt to Cooke, the great singer and writer who preceded him in the American soul tradition.

Sadly, like Cooke, Redding was not to enjoy a long life. He died in 1967 in a plane crash, shortly after a performance at the Monterey Pop Festival that suggested he had the capacity to connect with a broader audience (i.e., white hippies). Fortunately for the world, he left us *Otis Blue*, a record made in the space of a month that demonstrated the rare sound of a focused, razor-sharp performer at the zenith of his powers. There isn't a bad track on it.   Q.S.

Back in Black

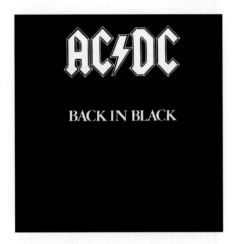

You put on *Back in Black* and you're sixteen years old, you're getting something. You know you're getting something for sure.

—JON BON JOVI

In many ways, AC/DC's magnum opus, *Back in Black*, appeared just as heavy metal, a genre that had already reached premature "dinosaur" status after only a decade, was standing at the crossroads between obsolescence and full-blown revival. Along with Van Halen, AC/DC were the first metal band to grasp the high-energy implications of punk. Whereas most heavy-metal acts were slowing down to dinosaur tempo and playing incomprehensibly long solos, both Halen and DC jacked up the energy level and constricted their songs into more pop-oriented blasts. The end result was a renewed vitality for metal that, along with Motorhead and the first two solo albums by Ozzy Osbourne, introduced a whole generation to the form, eventually resulting in the punk-metal crossover personified by Metallica and others. But whereas Halen soon succumbed to cheerleader-like wimpiness with "Jump," AC/DC continued to thud on in the same impeccably ham-handed manner right up through the next decade, varying their unmistakable plunder not one iota.

The circumstances of *Back in Black* would've deterred a band less oblivious than AC/DC. When

82

ATLANTIC
1980

Brian Johnson:
vocals

**Angus Young,
Malcolm Young:**
guitars

Cliff Williams:
bass

Phil Rudd:
drums

Produced by
Robert John
"Mutt" Lange

original lead singer Bon Scott OD'd on alcohol just as the band was getting their first taste of American success in 1979, a more sober unit might've called it quits, or at least taken a few months off to regroup. However, AC/DC had always lived on the edge, from their origins as a blues-rock bar band in their native Australia to the hellion heavy-metal unit they'd become by the time Scott kicked the bucket. In the face of tragedy, the best option appeared to be to soldier on. Recruiting singer-screamer Brian Johnson from another Aussie band, Geordie, and relocating to England, AC/DC kept any hint of remorsefulness close to the cuff, and plunged headlong into thunderous aplomb.

Recorded quickly in the spring of 1980, *Back in Black* hit the stands that summer and showed a band that was back with a vengeance. As the ominous clanging bells that open "Hell's Bells" demonstrated, AC/DC were hardly trying to atone for past sins. Johnson had learned to emulate Scott's guttural yowl perfectly, and, if anything, they'd beefed up the guitar sound even more. Credit this to producer John "Mutt" Lange, who began working with the band on *Highway to Hell,* crafting a more high-energy attack than their earlier, more blues-oriented albums. He understood that the band's sonic force rested on the harmonious interplay of all its elements—the guitars were compacted into a singular statement of rhythmic efficiency, the rhythm section provided the thunderhorse overdrive, and vocalist Johnson bellowed and brayed like the most unhinged practitioner of bluesy top-man dynamics since vintage Robert Plant. The end result was a sonic firestorm that not only was immensely powerful, but popular as well—by the year's end, AC/DC had managed the incredible feat of placing an actual heavy-metal song into the Top 40 ("You Shook Me All Night Long" made number thirty-four on the *Billboard* charts). The production of *Back in Black* was so influential that, to this day, producers still use it as the de facto paint-by-numbers guidebook for how a hard-rock record should sound. J.S.H.

Marquee Moon

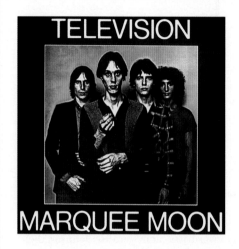

Verlaine's singing . . . seemed to straddle a line between panic and exhilaration, the whole song tumbling forth in a giddy, ass-over-teakettle rush.

I had a roommate obsessed with *Marquee Moon*. The title song especially, with its metronomic drumbeat, its pulsing, two-note bass, all ten minutes of it bleeding through the thin wall separating the living room from my bed. I hated it, God I hated it: that shrill repeating guitar riff, and Tom Verlaine's thyroidal singing, or "singing," since it sounded more like the protest of a neck-wrung hen. I was getting over something—a headache, a hangover, a bad girl experience—and that song, that song, was trying to stop me. I went into the living room, finally, while my roommate was out. I thought I'd hide the record, bury it somewhere he wouldn't find it, at least for a while. I held it in my hands, and— stopped. The cover art, Robert Mapplethorpe's photograph, showed four men, frozen and haloed in a spooky bluish glow. They looked like statues, and at the same time like flesh made supra-real; they were still, and yet they were moving; the man at the picture's center—Verlaine—had gigantic hands, and a swan-like hauteur. So arresting was this image, I had to play the record immediately, whether I'd hated it thus far or no. And as soon as the needle touched down, the chiming, fire-alarm guitar of "See No Evil" came leaping out of the speakers, I was transported. The record made sense to me, as it hadn't heard casually, filtered through a wall. Billy Ficca's careening drumming, Verlaine and Richard Lloyd's immaculate, interlocking guitars, and—especially, all of a sudden—Verlaine's singing. Which seemed to straddle a line between panic and exhilaration, the whole song tumbling forth in a giddy, ass-over-tea-kettle rush. Followed by the cascading, koan-like "Venus," the taut, spring-wound "Friction," and at last, my *bête noire,* "Marquee Moon." Which this time, at long last, caught me. With a guitar solo—a solo, although I'd spent my entire adolescence yawning in secret over the heavy indulgences of the rock guitar solo before punk rock

ELEKTRA
1977
Tom Verlaine:
guitar, keyboards, vocals
Richard Lloyd:
guitar, vocals
Fred Smith:
bass, vocals
Billy Ficca:
drums
Produced by
Tom Verlaine, Andy Johns

excused me from such a thing—or rather, two of them. First Richard Lloyd's concise, spiky, over-and-out break, and then Verlaine's. Which stammers, glimmers, spirals, and soars: a sound so exultant it is more like the greatest transcendental jazz (Coltrane, Albert Ayler, Pharoah Sanders) than any "rock" sound I have ever heard. By the time it ended, with one jubilant, pealing wave after another and then a return to that same rocksteady pulse I'd initially detested, I was goose-pimpled all over, and ready to hear it again.

Months would pass before I could even bring myself to flip the album over. And be no less astonished by the marvels of side two: the angular pop of "Elevation," the stop-start playfulness of "Prove It," the stately and exquisite "Guiding Light." To this day, I remain completely in the record's thrall, mesmerized by its marriage of passion and detachment, the latter just enough to ensure the former never wears out. I cannot imagine my—or anyone's—collection complete without it. M.S.

Graceland

Graceland *sounded like nothing most of America had ever heard before—and, perhaps surprisingly, thrust Simon back onto the pop music map in a big way.*

Very few artists within pop music get their second (or third) wind in their mid-forties. Even fewer forty-something artists are able to score a hit single with a song poking fun at middle age. An even rarer artist is the one who is able to introduce an unfamiliar form of music to a mass audience. But Paul Simon pulled off all of the above with *Graceland*.

After the lukewarm commercial response received by his underrated 1983 album *Hearts and Bones*, Simon looked to music outside of the American/British pop-rock spectrum for inspiration (as he had with Jamaican reggae on his first post–Simon & Garfunkel album, 1972's *Paul Simon*). This time, he had been turned on to an album called *Gumboots: Accordion Jive Hits, Volume II.* "It sounded vaguely like fifties rock & roll," Simon commented. "It was very 'up,' very happy music—familiar and foreign sounding at the same time." The music, as Simon discovered, was the "township jive" of Soweto, South Africa, also known as *mbaqanga*. Eventually, Simon and longtime collaborator Roy Halee flew to Johannesburg, South Africa, to record tracks with some of his favorite *mbaqanga* artists. Later, he took the tracks back to the United States, where he added to them with the help of, among others, guitar wizard Adrian Belew, the Everly Brothers, and Linda Ronstadt.

Graceland sounded like nothing most of America had ever heard before—and, perhaps surprisingly, thrust Simon back onto the pop music map in a big way. The album was introduced to the public via the single "You Can Call Me Al," which featured Simon's conversa-

WARNER BROS.
1986
Paul Simon:
vocals, guitar,
synclavier, six-string
electric bass
**Various Additional
Musicians**

Produced by
Paul Simon

tional/storytelling lyrics combined with exotic rhythms and an irresistible horn line. By 1986, of course, MTV was in full effect, and Simon had a deceptively simple video for the song—featuring nothing more than him and Chevy Chase hilariously lip-synching—that introduced him to a new generation of music fans. It is safe to say that the video music channel hasn't given much play to many other singles that dealt with such midlife issues as getting "soft in the middle" or wondering "who will be my role model, now that my role model is gone."

Surprisingly, the album got Simon blacklisted by the United Nations. The feeling was that Simon had broken a cultural boycott of South Africa (still in the throes of apartheid). Eventually, the U.N. saw that Simon had only (successfully) tried to expose the music of South Africa to the rest of the world, and eventually removed him from their blacklist. It all ended well: *Graceland* would win an Album of the Year Grammy, while the title track took Record of the Year.   B.I.

Abraxas

Santana were the pioneers of Latin rock, and their polyrhythmic stew combined with Carlos Santana's intense *Bolero*-like guitar soloing made them heroes to progressives of every race in the late sixties and early seventies. *Abraxas*, their second album, was where they really came into their own—the percussive forays, hypnotic guitar, and Latin rhythms inaugurated on their debut were driven to new heights by an expanded rhythm section and more focused songwriting. Santana, who were an oddity in 1969, became popular with *Abraxas* and brought the simmering sounds of

the Latin ghetto into the mainstream. But along with it, they also carried hints of very professional-styled white rock, mostly courtesy of keyboardist Greg Rolie (who later went on to form Journey), who wrote the more conventional rock ballads like "Mother's Daughter" and "Hope You're Feeling Better." This gave Santana the proper mix of ethnic influences to be successful on virtually every level—both as a pop success and as progressive innovators.

In the midst of the swirling Afro-Cuban rhythms that adorn *Abraxas*, there are traces of blues, jazz, and psychedelic rock. A perfect example is their adaptation of Fleetwood Mac's "Black Magic Woman"—in the hands of the Mac it was a conventional blues, but in the hands of Santana it became a strenuous exorcism of raw passion and intensity. The guitar solo burned all over the airwaves for months, sealing Santana's fate in classic-rock heaven for ever after. "Oye Como Va," a cover of a Tito Puente song, was similarly transformed into a hammering riff complete with greasy organ learned in the dives of Oakland where the band earned its chops. Not surprisingly, it followed "Black Magic Woman" up the charts. Almost as if to ascertain its basic garage-band origins, years later, Olympia indie-punk realists Beat Happening would lift the riff exactly for "Redhead Walking."

The songs "Incident at Neshabur" and "Samba Pa Ti" were Santana's attempts at straight-up progressiveness, in this case the kind of noodling fusion that was being practiced by people like John McLaughlin, Weather Report,

COLUMBIA
1970
Carlos Santana:
guitar
**Jose Chepitas Areas,
Rico Reyes:**
percussion
Greg Rolie:
vocals, keyboards
Michael Shrieve:
drums
Mike Carabello:
percussion
Albert Gianquinto:
piano
David Brown:
bass
Produced by
Carlos Santana

and Herbie Hancock (all by-products of Miles Davis's innovations on *Bitches Brew,* actually). Over outstretched polyrhythms provided by the band's well-stocked percussive section, guitars and keyboards construct a mosaic of percolating precision. Santana himself would pursue this direction further, both within the band construct as well as with his own collaborations with people like McLaughlin and Buddy Miles. However, it's questionable whether he would ever match the Latin-jazz-rock fusion perfected on *Abraxas.*

The cover was quite an eyeful as well, with its slightly-more-obscene-than-*National Geographic* nude woman reclined on the cover and liner notes like "we called her bitch and whore," which made a few hippies horny back in the day and proved that these were *definitely* the days before Carlos Santana's own conversion to Sri Chimnoy—which is probably why *Abraxas* is the group's best album: It's a sinner's serenade as hot-blooded as a Latin sundown, a regular pagan's feast.   J.S.H.

Quadrophenia

To understand *Quadrophenia*, it helps to know something about the Mods. A British youth cult in the early-to-mid-sixties, the Mods lived for snappy clothes, Italian motor scooters, amphetamines, and American R&B. Their archrivals were the

Rockers—leather-clad, Harley-driving street toughs—and the two gangs clashed frequently at seaside resorts on England's south coast. The Who was a Mod band in its formative years, and when, in the early seventies, the group's main songwriter Pete Townshend was searching for a new "rock opera" concept to follow the wildly successful *Tommy* and the aborted *Lifehouse* (portions of which were recycled for *Who's Next*), he found himself drawn to telling a story of that era. In the process, he created a work of art with universal appeal.

Quadrophenia's central character, Jimmy, is a Mod whose life has crumbled around him. He returns to Brighton, scene of one of the great Mod/Rocker riots, only to find that the "ace face" who led the charge is a lowly bell-boy at a local hotel. The plot line is even more fragmented than *Tommy*'s, and the notion that Jimmy is "quadrophenic," split into four different selves, is poorly developed. But Townshend's gut-wrenching songs—"The Real Me," "Cut My Hair," "Sea and Sand," "Love, Reign O'er Me"—make up for these deficiencies. Anyone who's longed to be part of a group, anyone who's felt turned off by society—anyone, in short, who's ever been a teenager—can identify with *Quadrophenia*'s sentiments.

The Who delivers those sentiments with vigor aplenty. Roger Daltrey's snarling vocals, Townshend's fluid guitar and keyboard work, John Entwistle's virtuosic bass and horn playing, and Keith Moon's over-the-top drumming bespeak a band at the height of its powers. Tracks like "5:15" and "Drowned" rock with all the force of a turbo-charged steamroller, while the album's two instrumentals, "Quadrophenia" and "The Rock," blend the four themes representing Jimmy's four personalities with a near-symphonic majesty. Yes, it helps to know something about the Mods to appreciate *Quadrophenia*, but it's not necessary; when music hits this hard, the difference between a Vespa and a Lambretta fades into insignificance.　M.R.

MCA
1973
Roger Daltrey:
vocals
Pete Townshend:
guitars, keyboards,
vocals
John Entwistle:
bass, horns, vocals
Keith Moon:
drums, percussion,
vocals
Produced by
the Who

Disraeli Gears

ATCO
1967
Eric Clapton:
guitar, vocals
Jack Bruce:
bass, vocals
Ginger Baker:
drums
Produced by
Felix Pappalardi

In the sixties, the precedent set by the Beatles, Bob Dylan (and, to a lesser extent, the Rolling Stones) demanded that each album a group or artist released was actually a step further along the path of their musical development. It was the era when each album was supposed to top the last.

For a rock band, they were pioneering, and the implication of their name introduced a new kind of arrogance that would have a profound impact on all subsequent lordly proceedings.

What this signified was a full-blown renaissance in the name of rock 'n' roll, and Cream was right in the middle of it.

When the trio debuted in England in 1966 they astounded audiences with not only their volume but also their strenuous renditions of blues classics like "I'm So Glad" and "Spoonful," which sometimes stretched into twenty-minute improvisations. For a rock band, they were pioneering, and the implication of their name—the "cream of the crop" of Britain's new generation of rock musicians—introduced a new kind of arrogance that would have a profound impact on all subsequent lordly proceedings (Led Zeppelin comes immediately to mind). Furthermore, along with the Jimi Hendrix Experience, who debuted around the same time and carried with them a lot of the same lofty concepts and attitudes, Cream was responsible for inventing the classic rock "power trio," an idea that would sweep the world in a few years' time in the form of such popular acts as Blue Cheer, Mountain, Grand Funk Railroad, and ZZ Top.

As far as the group's exulted reputation went, it wasn't entirely unjustified: Eric Clapton had been the whiz-kid guitarist who quit the Yardbirds over issues of purity and had proceeded to earn a rep as one of Britain's most incendiary fretboard-burners in John Mayall's Bluesbreakers; meanwhile, bassist Jack Bruce and drummer Ginger Baker—both veterans of the pioneering Brit-blues finishing school, the Graham Bond Organization—were responsible for elevating the rock rhythm section into a more flexible and creative tool than the largely beat-keeping maneuvers that had previously been the norm. However, surprisingly enough, despite the massive hype, the group's first album, *Fresh Cream*, while a worthy showcase for the group's estimable talents, tended to focus on shorter and more concise material than what they played live.

While *Disraeli Gears*, the band's second album, didn't really exceed the boundaries of accepted song structure as far as lengthy improvisation went (the group would tackle that on their next album, *Wheels of Fire*, complete with the side-long "Spoonful" and Ginger Baker's ill-fated drum solo "Toad"), it showed a new more riff-oriented direction for Cream that would prove to be incredibly influential in the birth of heavy metal a couple of years later. From the opening notes of "Strange Brew," it was obvious that the group was establishing an exciting groove. This new more organic looseness could perhaps also be attributed to the fact that Cream recorded the album in New York with the help of producer Felix Pappalardi (who'd later become the bass player in the Cream-influenced power trio, Mountain) and veteran Atlantic records engineer Tom Dowd, whose previous work had included such soul geniuses as Otis Redding and Aretha Franklin. Dowd's input no doubt gave *Disraeli Gears* an earthier groove that more easily translated to American success than the somewhat stodgy veneer of their debut album. Along with Buffalo Springfield, Cream was the first white rock band to be signed to Atlantic, which gave the already-be-knighted trio yet another feather in their caps.

Like the Doors's first album, Jefferson Airplane's *Surrealistic Pillow,* and the Beatles's *Sgt. Pepper's Lonely Hearts Club Band, Disraeli Gears* was one of those albums that helped define the pivotal year 1967. Songs like "Swlabr," "Strange Brew," and "Tales of Brave Ulysses" suggested that great changes were a-brew for the whole field of rock, with their nascent blend of psychedelic and heavy metal influences. And speaking of heavy metal, the classic "Sunshine of Your Love," a Top 10 hit, was a riff-rock prototype that set the stage for such future finger-exercises as Deep Purple's "Smoke on the Water" and Aerosmith's "Walk This Way" in the annals of ambling guitarists everywhere. Hell, it was so heavy even Hendrix saw fit to cover it.

The Hieronymus Bosch–influenced cover, with its maddening Technicolor collage, no doubt inspired as many freak-outs as the music itself. If there were one LP to sock away into a time capsule so that future generations might understand the whole naive nature of psychedelia—as well as the whole rock coming-of-age process—*Disraeli Gears* would be a likely candidate. Do 'em a favor and toss in a hit of blotter acid as well. J.S.H.

Remain in Light

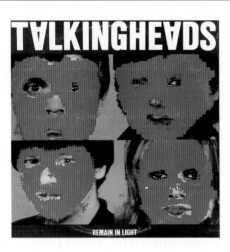

I was high on a hill—and high otherwise besides, on some potent skunk weed—looking down at the lights of Los Angeles, somewhere near the crest of Mulholland Drive. My friend who was older, and responsible for turning me on to all sorts of things (though it was *my* pot we'd been smoking), nodded his head sagely and said, "Check this out," while fiddling with his little Honda's tape deck. He was a sophisticate, lately graduated from Berkeley, a kind of older-brother figure, while I was still in high school. The song he made me listen to was "The Great Curve," off

Remain in Light. I'd known the Talking Heads largely through "Psycho Killer," the geeky, adenoidal near-novelty hit (it wasn't, but I might have been forgiven for thinking it was) off their first album, *Talking Heads '77*. This was different. And how. A fresh, frenetic, African-funk beat. A heavy, art-metal, Hendrix-on-the-moon guitar solo. Fractured, half-chanted lyrics: David Byrne had ditched his early, mannerist quirkiness for something even stranger, a radical alienation that might've appealed to any adolescent, let alone a stoned one. I suppose teenagers had been having this experience—that of having one's mind blown, I mean—ever since Bob Dylan first plugged in. This was it for me, though. I bought my own copy the next day and played it over and over, with alarmed fascination; the electro-treated frenzy of "Born Under Punches," the angular shuffle of "Houses in Motion." The creepy, inscrutable recitative "Seen and Not Seen."

When my living room was outfitted with a brand-new cable station called MTV, I switched it on for the first time and caught Byrne's spasmodic, panicked pantomime to "Once in a Lifetime," a perfect enactment of the song's description of suburban estrangement and alarm. For years I saw people imitate that anxious arm-chop, whatever it was that Byrne was up to in that video. It seemed impossibly fresh, as this was still some time before Paul Simon and who knows who else—innumerable artists including Byrne himself—began ransacking Africa and South Amer-

SIRE
1980
David Byrne:
bass, guitar, keyboards, percussion, vocals, voices
Tina Weymouth:
bass, keyboards, percussion
Chris Weymouth:
drums, keyboards, percussion
Jerry Harrison:
bass, guitar, keyboards, percussion, vocals
Adrian Belew:
guitar
Brian Eno:
bass, guitar, keyboards, percussion, synthesizer, vocals, voices
Nona Hendryx:
vocals, voices
Robert Palmer, Jose Rossy:
percusssion
Produced by
Brian Eno

ica, discovering and importing self-consciously "exotic" sounds. This was self-consciousness itself, in fact, expressed miraculously through improbably-congruous chattering drums and Fela-like, call-and-response vocals. It shouldn't have worked, and yet, in its blend of white-guy hypertension and tribal looseness, it worked perfectly. Parts of the album are gorgeous—"Listening Wind," for instance—while others, such as the spooked crawl of "The Overload," are a paranoiac's dream, or nightmare. Most of the album, indeed, is both. This was music that took me somewhere, and prepared *me* for some of the sounds that may have prepared *it:* Funkadelic's *Maggot Brain*, and Miles Davis's *Bitches Brew.* (Both, also, introduced to me that night. Some night.) Like those albums, *Remain in Light* could be said to be "head music." But also, and perhaps even more than the band's subsequent releases, with an unexpected warmth, and deep, deep soul. M.S.

89

Layla & Other Assorted Love Songs

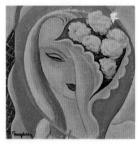

If you'd been Eric Clapton during the period that encompassed 1969–70, chances are you would've been tired. During that time, Clapton claimed membership—however fleeting the duration—in more than a few reputable rock outfits: Blind Faith, the Plastic Ono Band, Delaney & Bonnie, and finally Derek & the Dominoes. The last was actually an offshoot of the period spent on the road with Delaney & Bonnie, a roughshod hippie honky-tonk band from which he snatched drummer Jim Gordon, bassist Carl Radle, and keyboardist Bobby Whitlock, and the Dominoes they became. The band became Clapton's attempt to continue the kind of Southern roots–finding revelation that playing with Americans Delaney and Bonnie had provided, and to reconcile his spiritual connection with the American South that had given birth to Clapton's beloved blues.

Finding road-seasoned counterparts in the rhythm section of Radle and Gordon helped Clapton unfurl some of his most impassioned solos since the days when he was striving for blues purism in John Mayall's Bluesbreakers, before

the bombastic—and admittedly at times brilliant—proto-metal attack of Cream. But the deciding factor on this album's immortality rested solely on the fact that, during the second week of recording, Duane Allman joined the proceedings on slide guitar. He was at the time the rising star of the Allman Brothers Band, and Duane's presence ascertained that *Layla* was destined to become one of the all-time classic dual-guitar albums.

On the title cut, "Layla," the two guitarists go at one another with whipping frenzy as Clapton, who sounds as if he's performing a vocal exorcism, states his impassioned plea to the unrequited woman of his desires (whom everyone later learned was actually George Harrison's wife, Patti). Meanwhile, versions of Jimi Hendrix's "Little Wing" and Freddie King's "Have You Ever Loved a Woman" are convincing performances that take on a life of their own, as does the majestic "Bell Bottom Blues," which casts its shadow over the rest of this set with arching grace. *Layla* is a worthy exemplar of blues power as well as a kind of self-fulfilling prophecy.　J.S.H.

ATCO
1970
Eric Clapton:
guitar, vocals
Duane Allman:
guitar
Carl Radle:
bass
Bobby Whitlock:
keyboards, guitars, vocals
Jim Gordon:
drums
Produced by
Tom Dowd

Tommy

90

The Beatles' *Sgt. Pepper's Lonely Hearts Club Band*, released in 1967, changed the nature of album-making forever. Surely, the Who's *Tommy* was one of the most challenging opuses to appear in its wake. Pete Townshend had begun to germinate his concept of a "rock opera" a couple of years previously—but it was only the ever-expansive freedom that musicians and composers experienced in the late sixties that enabled him to pursue his concept to a logical conclusion. Therefore *Tommy* was important for two reasons: It established Townshend as one of the major rock composers of the day, and it helped expand the possibilities of what could be done in the name of rock album-making.

Spreading over two LPs, the album told the story of a deaf, dumb, and blind boy who, because of his telepathic relationship with a pinball machine, becomes a Messiah for the New Age. It was a concept fraught with everything from drippy hippie idealism to New Age pretenses, but it worked because of the strength of the music. The band, who'd been gaining popularity in the States ever since their cataclysmic performance at the Monterey Pop Festival (and they were soon to play Woodstock), were entering their most productive phase, similar to what the Stones were doing at the time. It all had to do with the previously inconceivable concept of "maturity" in rock 'n' roll. The Who were among the architects of this growth process, and *Tommy* represents the turning point in the band's career in both an artistic and commercial sense.

Being a two-record set, there's some dross on *Tommy*. But the truly outstanding performances—"Amazing Journey," "Christmas," "Go to the Mirror," "I'm Free," and "We're Not Gonna Take It"—are riffing monstrosities of ample hard-rock prowess (the Who's specialty in a nutshell). Townshend's "The Acid Queen," on which he handles the lead vocal, is one of his most stunning compositions—a frightening ode to LSD phrased in seductive metaphors.

What the Who have always been about—in fact, what they helped perfect in the rock context—was the power of each individual player and the way that power can be combined into a propulsive dynamic. On *Tommy* they established this dynamic in resounding waves that would resonate for years to come. J.S.H.

DECCA
1969
Peter Townshend:
guitar, keyboard, vocals
Roger Daltrey:
vocals
John Entwistle:
bass, french horn, vocals
Keith Moon:
drums, vocals
Produced by
Kit Lambert

So

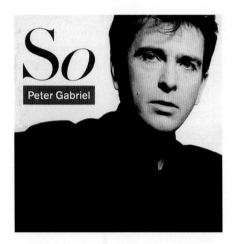

It was the album that introduced Peter Gabriel to the world. Sure, he was well known in rock circles as the original singer in Genesis, and his first four solo albums had carved him a comfortable niche as a left-of-center artist with a rabid cult following. But, with 1986's *So*, Gabriel became one of the most popular recording artists in the world.

Gabriel had, of course, enjoyed a number of hits before—"Biko," "Games Without Frontiers," and "Shock the Monkey"—but none had the crossover appeal of *So*'s first single, the funky "Sledgehammer," a number-one hit in the U.S.

The song's success was aided by the innovative claymation video, which collected nine "Moonmen" at the 1987 Video Music Awards. But according to Gabriel's ubiquitous bassist, Tony Levin, Gabriel often consciously aimed away from the pop arena.

"I have always noticed that if a piece sounds quite 'accessible' or 'radio friendly,' Peter would change it! All his music is well thought out and well crafted, but if he thought that people might think he was 'trying to have a hit,' or even a single, he would alter it."

91

Indeed, Levin recalls that "Sledgehammer" wasn't originally recorded for inclusion on *So* at all.

"What happened with 'Sledgehammer,' I believe, is that it was tagged on the end of the sessions—not really to be on *So*, but on a future album. We recorded it on the last night of the sessions. So, my theory is, that when they decided to use it on the album, even though it was pretty radio friendly, Peter didn't have *time* to change it!"

"Big Time," an even funkier track, was a number-eight hit. Aspiring bass players may have played their fingers bloody trying to figure out the lightning-quick riff that starts the song. In fact, for the riff in question, Levin's fingers didn't touch his bass strings at all: "When I heard the theme of the song, it just occurred to me that having [drummer] Jerry [Marotta] drum a pattern on my strings might be worth trying." The experiment worked, but when Gabriel and company hit the road, they wanted to replicate the sound without pulling Marotta away from the drums. At first Levin used a drumstick to bang notes out on his bass; eventually, though,

GEFFEN
1985
Peter Gabriel:
drums, flute, keyboards, percussion, piano, synthesizer, vocals
Various musicians
Produced by
Peter Gabriel, Chris Hughes, Daniel Lanois

Gabriel, Levin, and bass tech Andy Moore came up with the idea to attach chopped-down drum sticks to Levin's fingers. After refining the original rough design, Levin created patented "Funk Fingers," which he would later sell on his Web site.

Not all the songs on *So* yielded such ingenious inventions, nor did they need to. Two of the songs featured collaborations with other cult-level singers: Kate Bush duetted with Gabriel on the gorgeous "Don't Give Up." Senegalese singer Youssou N'Dour, meanwhile, provided backing vocals on "In Your Eyes," one of the most popular love songs of the late eighties and nineties. (Generation X-ers will never forget the iconic image from the 1989 Cameron Crowe drama, *Say Anything*, of a rain-drenched Lloyd Dobler [played by John Cusack] holding a boombox over his head, playing "In Your Eyes," in an effort to make amends with his girlfriend.)

Peter Gabriel has had the knack over the years of taking creative, challenging ideas and weaving them into unforgettable pop songs, but it never worked quite as well as it did on *So*.   B.I.

92

Murmur

Their first full-length album established REM as one of the few groups in the early eighties capable of creating a new sound and being able to sustain it through the long-playing medium. *Murmur* was crafted like the records of yore, by groups like the Beatles, the Byrds, and the Beach Boys: a free-flowing entity that, while not exactly thematic in intent, nevertheless came together as if constructed with some idea of unity in mind.

REM's sound was a harmonious hybrid of those influences and many others. They fell into line with groups inspired by punk's spirit but unwilling to forsake their classic rock roots. In this sense, they were one of the first groups to expand on the D.I.Y. spirit in a way that was still familiar enough not to scare off radio programmers. The consummate college rock band, REM demonstrated the enormous potential of that audience. People forget how stifling the climate of the eighties was. To kids on campuses all over America, REM was a bright spot on an otherwise ultra-conformist horizon.

Beginning with the clarion burst of "Radio Free Europe," which combined Byrdsian jangle with the echoey denseness of Echo

& the Bunnymen, *Murmur* was intelligent, evocative, and thought-provoking. "Pilgrimage" created a starkly moving portrait of measured precision. It was a less cathartic sound than punk, but one no less wrought with disturbing themes and images. "Moral Kiosk" created a haunting portrait of alienation, a common theme for Michael Stipe whose ironic detachment in songs like "Talk About the Passion" became the prototype for post-everything ideology. Kurt Cobain was one of the many listening. His mumbly vocal style was a direct descendent of Stipe's.

The ironic aspects of REM can't be underestimated, nor were these calculating traits strictly confined to their lyrical endeavors—there were also the subtle changes of melody in songs like "Sitting Still" that made them memorable for years to come. As the years passed, it would only get better, until 1987, when standing on the cusp of total eighties consciousness, they would pen perhaps the ultimate post-everything ditty "The End of the World (As We Know It)," which summed up the era better than anything. The germination for this mastery began with *Murmur*.   J . S . H .

I.R.S.
1983

Michael Stipe:
vocals

Bill Berry:
drums

Mike Mills:
bass

Peter Buck:
guitar

Produced by:
Don Dixon

Bookends

"Time it was, and what a time it was, it was." With these, the opening words of "Bookends Theme," Paul Simon and Art Garfunkel bid a tender adieu to the Age of America. As the sixties spiraled toward a violent climax, the innocence of the postwar years was gone forever, leaving only memories and the sobering chill of autumn. It is this sense of nostalgia, vain hope, and withered dreams that Simon & Garfunkel capture so adroitly on *Bookends*. From the tale of a young couple's long-distance bus journey in "America" to the portrait of a disillusioned middle-aged woman in "Mrs. Robinson" (who has little in common with her namesake in *The Graduate*, the film in which the song was first heard), Simon & Garfunkel's fourth album is a bittersweet shot of melancholy.

Although it sounds like a preplanned, tightly wrought song cycle, *Bookends* is actually a hodgepodge of tracks, the oldest of which, "A Hazy Shade of Winter," was recorded more than a year and a half before the album's release. But thematically, its twelve songs fit together perfectly. And their complex musical arrangements stretch the duo's "folk" style in new directions; listen to the lachrymose strings on "Old Friends," the blaring horns on "Fakin' It," or the raspy Moog synthesizer on "Save the Life of My Child."

In his later years, Paul Simon has turned up his nose at many of the songs he wrote during the Simon & Garfunkel era. He's expressed disdain for the way they overreach, for the obviousness of their adolescent pretensions. Listening to *Bookends*, it's difficult to share his perspective. Certainly the music has its dated, overprecious moments, but at its core, what it has to tell us remains valid. We still feel a sense of longing for some distant time in the past when we believed everything was right. People are still steering their cars down the New Jersey Turnpike to look for America. Most importantly, the sophistication of Simon's melodies, his crystalline guitar playing, the way his voice blends with Garfunkel's in pure, peerless harmony—all these things have lost none of their power to bewitch.

M.R.

COLUMBIA
1968
Paul Simon:
vocals, guitars
Art Garfunkel:
vocals
Various guest musicians

Produced by
Paul Simon,
Art Garfunkel,
Roy Halee

OK Computer

"We are not going to make f***ing *The Bends II."* This was the statement that producer Nigel Godrich recalls Thom Yorke proclaiming during the recording sessions for *OK Computer*. It became the band's mantra. They had no intention of creating a sequel to their widely renowned sophomore album. On July 1, 1997, *OK Computer* was born—different, unique, fitter, happier, more productive. . . .

Godrich, who had worked on *The Bends* as the assistant to producer John Leckie, had witnessed Radiohead's difficulty trying to record within the confines of a windowless studio. With this in mind, Godrich listened to their sonic concerns. "We figure everything sounds great when we tape it in our room," he recalls them telling him. "We just want to capture that, you know. Help us get some gear together and just do it." Thus was born Canned Applause, a mobile recording unit that followed the band throughout the making of the album, from sessions in Radiohead's rehearsal space outside of Oxford (an old apple shed in the middle of a grove), to actress Jane Seymor's spacious manor outside of Bath, onto other temporary spaces that contained the sounds the band was looking for.

As far as how the songs came to be? "I stand by my claim that so much of it was an accident," says Godrich. The process is completely not by design but by accident. I mean we went around all the houses. At the time it seemed like we spent forever making it because we pretty much did everything, every possible way, because we could. We could afford the time to experiment."

Hard to believe that the genius of tracks like "Paranoid Android," "Exit music (For a Film)," "Subterranean Homesick Alien," and the rest of the tunes were all pieces of experiments fit together to create remarkable songs.

"Paranoid Android" can be the first example of this—a six-minute song with no chorus and complex time changes, proclaimed by Radiohead to be their own "Happiness Is a Warm Gun" (The Beatles). The song is actually the product of three and a half to four tracks that the band didn't know what to do with, so they were quilted together to make one. End result—their first single.

> **CAPITOL**
> 1997
> **Thom Yorke:**
> vocals, guitars
> **Jonny Greenwood:**
> guitars
> **Phil Selway:**
> drums
> **Ed O'Brien:**
> guitar, vocals
> **Colin Greenwood:**
> bass
> **Committed to tape by**
> Nigel Godrich with
> Radiohead

The haunting nature of "Exit Music" is another example of just how "lucky" the band can be. "You know something came out of a really typical, sort of potentially disastrous situation when everything is flying off the handle and people are getting upset. Something good comes from that energy." Here Godrich is referring to the ghostlike effect added to Thom Yorke's voice. The band had been having a tough couple of weeks and Yorke retreated into a new room in Seymour's house to privately record his vocals for the song. The spacious stone rooms within their sixteenth century recording space offered an organic reverb and Yorke had found the nook that provided the perfect echo for his voice.

If one listens closely, you can hear the rest of the genius that was discovered by chance, from the pieced-together portions at the end of "Karma Police" to the fun that Yorke was having one day on a Macintosh, creating "Fitter, Happier." Combine these together with Yorke's picturesque yet unsparing lyrics and you have an album like no other before it. H . S .

Private Dancer

The word is indomitable. She has that kind of spirit because it will not ever, ever, ever be overridden by anything else. It's just there. You cannot conquer it. —ROBERTA FLACK

Later in life I would learn her story and come to understand what the driving force for her comeback album really was.

Fishnet stockings, soulful red lips, and a mane fit for a lion: This will always be the image the not only beckons me back to the summer of 1984 on MTV but commands me to dutifully pay respect to the reigning queen of rock and soul. Tina Turner, with the release of *Private Dancer*, mounted perhaps the greatest comeback in the history of popular music. As a suburban teen, those images and desperate yearnings were unlike any other in the cauldron of testosterone found in the early eighties jungle of rock and pop. Not knowing what was fueling the passionate rejection of "What's Love Got to Do with It" or the lipstick-on-your-collar-for-a-dollar sorrow of "Private Dancer," I was drawn in by Tina's fist-in-the-air attitude. Later in life I would learn her story and come to understand what the driving force for her comeback album really was.

95

Her first single, "What's Love Got to Do with It," was her personal anthem of breaking free from former husband Ike Turner. With a chorus of "I've been thinking of a new direction / But I have to say / I've been thinking of my own protection / It scares me to feel this way," was not just an ironic tip of the hat but a bold statement that secured her place in music history as a solo artist, with an exclamation point. Tina delivered an unapologetic look at love and relationships. While she had boys young enough to be her grandkids breathless behind chainlink fences in the video, she got her message across by proving that she could stand firmly on her own two black stilettos.

"Better Be Good to Me" is the walloping finish of her one-two punch following "What's Love . . ." Tina takes no chances in a possible misunderstanding of her newfound independence. The boxing gloves are tied and ready for action. You can just see Tina raising her fist to Ike or any other ill-willing male as she snarls, " 'Cause I don't have the time / For your overloaded lies / You better be good to me." This is

CAPITOL
1984
Tina Turner:
Vocals
Various Musicians

Various Producers

possibly even scarier than her nostril-flaring role as the Acid Queen in *Tommy*.

Finishing the Top 10 triumvirate is "Private Dancer," written by Dire Straits front man Mark Knopfler. While the melody is sweet, the lyrics sting with thoughts of a rag-doll woman and her melancholy existence. Tina shimmied and sashayed her way up the charts for thirteen weeks with *Private Dancer*.

Al Green's "Let's Stay Together" has Tina singing a mixed-message classic in this hear-me-roar solo debut. It gives firm validity to an already taut package, as if Tina needed just that one safety net under her bold trapeze act. In the end, Tina's strong-footed acrobatic stunts were the pieces that stole center stage. An interesting addition to the album is the Bowie-penned "1984," in which our MVL (most valuable legs) mistress takes cues from Ziggy Stardust and George Orwell.

Private Dancer was Tina Tuner's pièce de résistance, proving to fans worldwide that she was no longer rolling down the river on Ike's raft, had booked her own ocean liner, and was quickly picking up passengers from coast to coast. R.B.

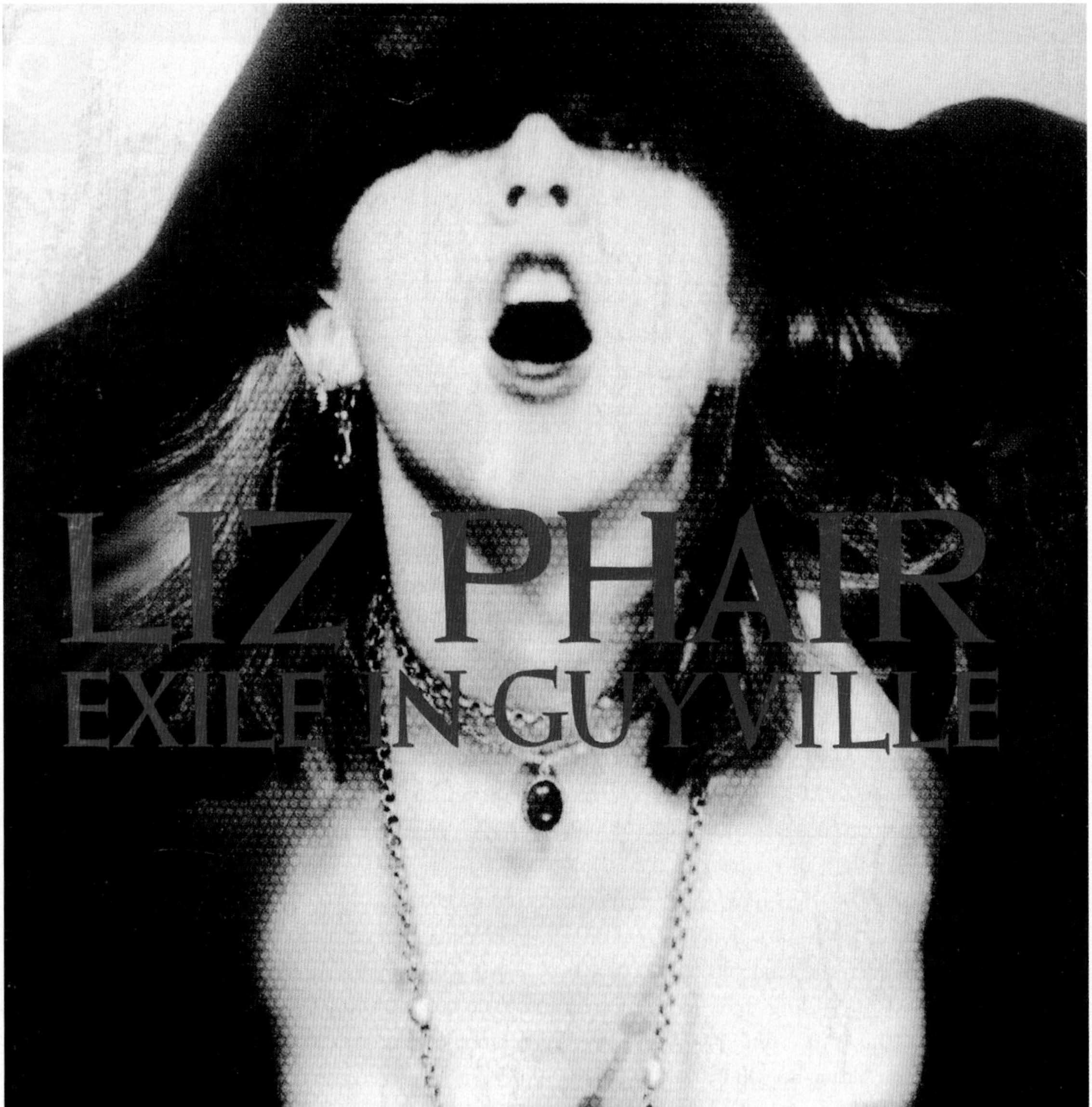
LIZ PHAIR
EXILE IN GUYVILLE

Exile in Guyville

96

It is fitting that Liz Phair first recorded many of the songs that would make up her eighteen-track opus *Exile in Guyville* after a less than fruitful postcollegiate move to the West Coast to pursue a career in fine art, and that she did so using a low-tech four-track recorder in her Chicago bedroom. The twenty-six-year old, middle-class Oberlin College grad unleashed her first effort in 1993, and with it took aim at the male-dominated rock 'n' roll scene with a track-by-track response to the Rolling Stones's canonized cock-rock epic *Exile on Main Street*. A record that stinks of ambition, sex, vulnerability, courage, humiliation, and hubris, *Exile in Guyville* plays like the contents of a smart chick's journal, settling once and for all that the nice girl next door can be anything but.

The story of Phair's path from boudoir songstress to brazen postmodern cover girl is that of indie rock lore: Bootlegs of two homespun demo tapes, appropriately dubbed *Girly Sounds*, circulated into the hands of record

MATADOR
1993
Liz Phair:
vocals, guitar, piano, bongos, hand claps
Brad Wood:
guitar, organ, synthesizer, bass, drums, percussion, background vocals
Casey Rice:
guitar, cymbal, hand claps, background vocals
John Casey Awsumb:
harmonica
Tony Marlotti:
bass
Tutti Jackson, O:
background vocals
Produced by
Liz Phair, Brad Wood

execs and landed the musician a deal with Matador. *Exile in Guyville* went on to be named Album of the Year by the *Village Voice* and *Spin;* the paradoxically pretty and sultry Phair landed on the covers of *Rolling Stone* and *Vogue.*

The triumphs of *Exile in Guyville* are many; the biggest, perhaps, is Phair's ability to seamlessly weave all of the album's accomplishments into a single, complex portrait of a single—and single-minded—woman. The persona she projects through the deeply personal narratives defies categorization; with each song she opens a window to reveal her true self, only to shut it quickly and open another, exposing an equally convincing and honest view into her soul. The message is clear: To understand this woman, whoever she is—Phair, or maybe your sister—you will have to view her from many angles, per-

> *A record that stinks of sex, vulnerability, courage, humiliation, and hubris,* Exile in Guyville *plays like the contents of a smart chick's journal, settling once and for all that the nice girl next door can be anything but.*

haps more than you have previously been asked to synthesize when considering the fairer sex.

The production of the album is appropriately spare, showcasing Phair's vocals that are alternately sweet, soulful, and self-consciously demure, shaky and unsure, sexual, furious and frank. But Phair's voice isn't particularly pleasing in any traditional sense; her consistently flat delivery indicates that her priority is not sounding pretty, but expressing her ideas in a signature style.

Like many, this woman craves companionship. "Fuck and Run" unabashedly proclaims the desire for a boyfriend and old-fashioned romance after countless one-night stands. Similarly, "Shatter" acknowledges the truth that after many ships pass in the night, some chance encounters run irrecoverably deep. Conversely, straight-up lust and desire are as much a part of a girl's needs as anyone's, and "Mesmerizing" and "Soap Star Joe" concede the irresistible and human need to captivate those we know aren't good for us. The shockingly frank "Flower" (written years before Alanis Morissette went down on anyone in a movie theater) uses falsetto-delivered words like "wet," "dick," and "suck," as well as the phrase "fresh young jimmy," to put a very fine point on a woman's desire to have sex with a man *right now*—perhaps (could it be?!) with a ferocity that would send him running home to his mother clutching his skivvies. In the same vein, "Girls! Girls! Girls!," fueled by its predatory baseline and deadpan delivery, plays against its title, making it plain that people of the female persuasion can go head-to-head in the arena of desire with someone of Mick Jagger's omnivorous libido any day of the week.

Backing up all of this are the tracks evidencing hard-won life experience, boy-related and otherwise. The guitar-heavy singles "6' 6"" and "Never Said" chronicle Phair as she faces down ill-fated paramours with a steely eye, while "Help Me Mary" finds Phair hoping her success will ultimately pierce those who doubt her talents. The heartbreaking, stripped-down "Divorce Song" relates a convoluted trip between lovers who have reached the end of the road.

The backbone of this album is its theme of a woman—simultaneously sexual, needy, and strong—moving through the world as an independent force. This idea is perhaps most precisely expressed in the penultimate track, "Stratford-On-Guy," which finds Phair on an airplane, backed by a looped, churning guitar, reclaiming and updating the traditionally male film noir narrative: She hovers above a cityscape, surrounded by blue-green smoke, finding that everything falls away in just the right cinematically inspired circumstance.

Liz Phair went on to get married and have a child, which proved fodder for subsequent creative efforts. Perhaps there is bliss through the fire. For the rest of us lonely hearts, there will always be *Exile*.   M.O.

97 Modern Sounds in Country & Western Music

A decade before Ray Charles cut this album, he'd already introduced the gospel influence into pop music via the records he'd made first for Swing Time and then the historic recordings he made for Atlantic, which, along with recordings made around the same time by people like James Brown and Sam Cooke, were responsible for inventing soul music. Born dirt-poor on a plantation in Georgia in a town where *everybody* went to

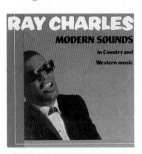

church, Charles was no stranger to the sanctified sounds of gospel, but, as he was careful to point out in interviews, being a product of the South, he was no stranger to country and western either (after all, while at Atlantic, he'd already recorded the Hank Snow classic "I'm Movin' On"). In this sense, it was inevitable that, just as he'd previously experimented with jazz idioms, Ray Charles would seek to incorporate these country influences into his music. While *Modern Sounds* was by no means a straight country album, it was enough of a departure from his ordinarily downhome sound to be his first number-one album. However, even in the midst of this mainstream success, Charles never lost his hardcore black following.

The reason for that can be found in this record's grooves. The choirlike accompaniment of the Raelettes adorns the million-selling hit single "I Can't Stop Loving You," adding a unique gospel twist to the Don Gibson tune, while his versions of Nashville standards like "Hey Good Looking" and "Bye Bye Love" retain a hint of his trademark soulfulness. The proceedings admittedly get schmaltzy at times, but Charles is a great interpreter and he transcends the commercial slickness that might have hurt a more compromising artist under such circumstances. It was Charles's idea to record this album, and far from being just a pawn in the hands of his new label, ABC, he was one of the first black artists to exercise artistic control over his own career. The miracle of *Modern Sounds* is that while it was one of the biggest-selling black albums up until that time, it was also one of the biggest-selling country ones. Which is why country artists like Willie Nelson and Buck Owens have continually cited Charles's influence. If the definition of a truly *great* artist is one who can transcend all categories, then Ray Charles definitely falls into that category. This album is part of the proof.　J.S.H.

ABC-PARAMOUNT
1962
Ray Charles:
vocals, piano, organ
David "Fathead" Newman:
saxophone
Produced by
Sid Feller

ABC

The Gary, Indiana, family fivesome may have been the first urban boy-band to cross over into mainstream culture with such stratospheric success.

First starting in their basement led by their taskmaster father, Joe, and then personally groomed by Motown Records president Berry Gordy, they spent five years honing their act before arriving in 1969 with the number-one smash "I Want You Back" from their debut disc *Diana Ross Presents the Jackson 5*.

But it was their sophomore effort, *ABC*, which contained their second and third consecutive number-one hits, "ABC" and "The Love You Save," which truly catapulted the group into the international spotlight.

Album cuts like "Don't Know Why I Love You" and "Never Had a Dream Come True" showcased Michael's natural talent as a versatile frontman and engaging performer, while allowing the other brothers to flex their own vocal skills. Overall, *ABC* is the Jackson 5's most formidable recording, showcasing the collective's infectious energy and undeniable pop presence. Later records would have hits of

their own like the saccharine-sweet ballad "I'll Be There" and the softly beguiling "Never Can Say Goodbye," but none can match the overall strength of *ABC*.

Released between the Golden Age of Soul and the funk fashions of the seventies, the Jackson 5's clean-cut image and catchier-than-thou tunes made them a very bankable part of the Motown hit machine. By the time the Jackson 5 story ran its bittersweet course, the teen heartthrobs had become a merchandiser's dream, rivaling KISS for the seemingly endless stream of products to which they could lend their likeness, and they had racked up over a dozen Top 40 hits.

The quintet would serve as the blueprint for the likes of New Edition and Boys II Men (and later, the Backstreet Boys and 'NSync), helping usher in an era where black pop bands were just as acceptable and triumphant as their blue-eyed counterparts.　N . M .

MOTOWN
1970

Jermaine Jackson:
vocals

Tito Jackson:
vocals

Marlon Jackson:
vocals

Jackie Jackson:
vocals

Michael Jackson:
vocals

Produced by
Leonard Caston,
Hal Davis,
Bobby Taylor

The B-52's

In the late seventies, the sight of B-52's girls Kate Pierson and Cindy Wilson frugging around on the set of *Fridays,* ABC's short-lived answer to *Saturday Night Live,* was a kind of culture shock that even the nihilistic urgings of punk hadn't prepared the world for. After years of hippie culture, and the whole back-to-nature plainness of mid-seventies superstars like the Eagles, Jackson Browne, and Neil Young, who downplayed the "glamour" quotient, something as flamboyantly camp as the B-52's was a direct affront to mainstream sensibilities. The essence of New Wave, the B-52's combined playful silliness with outright kitsch in a musical mix that was both propulsive and infectious. To many, this made them seem like a gimmick, but if critics had looked below the surface they would've discovered that the group had been part of Athens, Georgia's avant-garde long before that city became one of the first indie-rock capitals. Early versions of "52 Girls" and the classic "Rock Lobster," recorded for their own label, proved that the group was capable of straightforward punk aggression. The versions on *The B-52's*, while no less frenetic, were given considerably more depth by the titanic production style of Chris Blackwell, so much so that "Rock Lobster" actually became one of the first significant New Wave hits.

In many ways, the group was a perfect contradiction: With their beehive haircuts and covers of Petula Clark's "Downtown," they were hearkening back to a day and age when dancing was still the currency of rock 'n' roll, and this made them able to cash in on the danceable potential of New Wave before just about anyone else. At the same time, with Fred Schneider's mechanical-sounding voice and material like "Planet Clare" as well as the mutants-on-the-loose barrage of "Rock Lobster," they were nudging into a futuristic void that made them psychic allies with androids like Devo and Gary Numan. *The B-52's* was one of the first American New Wave albums to crack the Top 50, and it was on the strength of songs like "52 Girls," "Dance This Mess Around," "Lava," and "6060-842," which combined crazy rhythms

WARNER BROS.
1979
Fred Schneider:
vocals, keyboard, piano
Kate Pierson:
vocals, guitar, keyboard
Keith Strickland:
drums
Ricky Wilson:
guitar
Cindy Wilson:
vocals, tambourine
Produced by
Chris Blackwell

with absurd lyrics and the constant intertwining of complex male-female vocal harmonies. The fact that the two women in the group apparently existed on equal footing with their male counterparts helped set the stage for the whole inter-gender exchange of alternative rock, along with the group's ironic, campy sensibilities.

What few people realized at the time was that there was even a gay subtext—having been part of the whole post-Warhol scene, or what that amounted to in Georgia in the mid-seventies anyway, the group had adopted many of their camp aspects from the art underground. Which means along with *Beach Blanket Bingo* and other retro kitsch, there was also a little Robert Mapplethorpe thrown in. When Fred Schneider screams "here comes the bikini wail" in "Rock Lobster" in a voice that's only slightly to the right of Liberace it becomes evident that, far from a seventies version of the Archies, the B-52's were actually among the vanguard of the real velvet underground.
J.S.H.

Like a Prayer

When Madonna released *Like a Prayer*, she was already a household name. But with this album, the woman who would come to be recognized as a sexual revolutionary, chameleon of identity, and prognosticator of pop culture stepped forward with an album that let the world know she was a player. *Like a Prayer* is not a great record because every track on it is a masterpiece, or because it is a work of art from start to finish. It is a great album because it was here that the true identity of Madonna—role model, artist, and icon—began to rear its beautiful and ugly head.

The first single, "Like a Prayer," was accompanied by a much-discussed and controversial video in which Madonna danced in front of burning crosses and kissed an African American saint. The result: Pepsi canceled the sponsorship of her tour as well as a commercial contract, and the singer further cemented her now widely acknowledged flair for ruffling people's feathers and getting press while doing so. But the title track itself should not be discounted; its haunting intro builds infectiously to a supercharged, gospel-choir-infused chorus, resulting in a soulful and dance-friendly triumph. Another hit, the single girl anthem "Express Yourself," found the woman who seemed close to having everything shunning the ephemera of satin sheets, roses, and fast cars in favor of a communicative man. "Don't go for second best, put your love to the test," she advised women, adding, "You'd do much better, baby, on your own." "Cherish," an infectiously, hopelessly romantic pop song delivered with a light touch, invoked the iconic love-locked pair, Romeo and Juliet. Surprise: It too was a hit.

The tracks that didn't top the charts tend to be overlooked, but *Like a Prayer*'s strength extends beyond the radio-friendly hits, with songs that offer an emotionally exposed Madonna who is interested in producing music more than catchy pop confections. "Til Death Do Us Part" tells the story of a doomed, long-term, deeply soured marriage; "Promise to Try" is a spare and bittersweet ballad addressing the singer's childhood loss of her mother, and the powerful "Oh, Father" tells of a strained and complex relationship with another parental figure.

SIRE
1989
Madonna:
synthesizer, vocals
Various musicians

Produced by
Steven Bray, Patrick Leonard, Madonna

Most notably, it is on *Like a Prayer* that Madonna's sound, both vocally and lyrically, comes into its own. The high-pitched squeak found on the singer's earlier hits has departed, making way for a voice with range, soul, and heart. Even through the relatively slick production of the album, there are times when she sounds young and raw, and given all that she would eventually become, this is in its own way powerful.

Her gift for writing and delivering the straightforward lyric without apology emerges on the record as well. The lines of these songs are simple, and to the jaded, may seem unsophisticated: "Our luck is running out of time / You're not in love with me anymore" ("Til Death Do Us Part"), "I never felt so good about myself" ("Oh, Father"), "Don't forget that your family is gold" ("Keep It Together"), "You are my destiny" ("Cherish") are examples of *Like a Prayer*'s clear and uncomplicated lyrics. But these sentiments are the stuff of life, and through them, the artist Madonna connected with millions. M.O.

About the Authors

HARLAN COBEN is the *New York Times* bestselling author of *Tell No One* and *Gone for Good*. He has won the Edgar, Anthony, and Shamus Awards, and his books have been published in twenty-two languages thus far. His new novel, *No Second Chance*, will be released in April 2004. You can learn more about him at www.harlancoben.com

STUART COHN develops TV series for MTV News and Docs. He is a coauthor of *MTV Uncensored*.

When she's not DJing, record shopping, or thriftin' for pop culture artifacts, **RAQUEL BRUNO** is working on *Aquatulle* (an eighties pop culture magazine) which she founded in 1996 as an outlet for showcasing her and her friends' love for classic pop culture. Since then, she's put out one issue of *Aquatulle* every year. She's been written up in *Time Out New York*, *Bop* magazine, the *New York Times*, and even wrote a piece on Mr. Mister for *CMJ Monthly*'s "GeekLove!"

DAVID P. GALUSKI lives and writes in Providence, Rhode Island. His dream is to write a rock opera based on the works of Belle and Sebastian.

MICHAEL J. GARVEY is the Director of Music Programming and Production at VH1 Classic, the channel that presents music videos, concerts, and music specials from the sixties, seventies and eighties. The Massachusetts native has worked at VH1 for over nine years in music programming and production.

JOE S. HARRINGTON was born in Portland, Maine. Influenced by *Mad* magazine, Lester Bangs, and punk rock, he began writing record reviews for a hometown paper, *Sweet Potato*, before he even graduated from high school. Moving to Boston in the eighties, he freelanced widely for a variety of publications, including *High Times, Boston Rock, Raygun, Reflex, Wired, Lowell Sun, Boston Phoenix, Boston Globe, Rollerderby, New York Press*, and Amazon.com. Returning to Maine in 2000, he became the music critic for the *Casco Bay Weekly* in Portland while continuing to freelance for a wide variety of media outlets. His first book, *Sonic Cool: The Life & Death of Rock 'n' Roll*, was published by Hal Leonard in 2002.

JACOB HOYE is not a pseudonym. He believes the pyramids hold the key to understanding the history of civilization and that Bob Dylan should win the Nobel Prize for Literature.

BRIAN IVES is a producer for VH1 News and has worked for VH1 Radio, MTV2, MTV.com, Launch.com, and Concrete Marketing. He is also a freelance writer, and owns ninety-three of the one hundred albums in this book. He still can't believe that *not one* Neil Young solo album made the cut.

NEVIN MARTELL has published two books, *Dave Matthews Band: Music for the People*, and *Beck: The Art of Mutation*, and his work has appeared in *CMJ, Gear, Raygun*, and on RollingStone.com. He currently lives in New York City, where he divides his time between hardcore slacking and last-minute scrambling.

MIMI O'CONNOR lives and writes in Brooklyn. In 1983, she believed it was her destiny to marry Daryl Hall. She is no longer under that impression.

MAC RANDALL is the author of *Exit Music: The Radiohead Story*. A former senior editor at *Musician* magazine, he currently writes about music for a variety of publications, including the *New York Times, Rolling Stone*, the *New York Observer*, and *Guitar World*. He lives in New York City, and plays guitar in the instrumental rock trio Fuller.

JOHN REED is the author of *Snowball's Chance*, the controversial 9/11 updating of *Animal Farm*. His first novel was *A Still Small Voice*. His writing has appeared in *New York Press, Fat*, and *Open City*, among other publications. He lives and works in New York City.

COURTNEY REIMER spends her days rubbing elbows with the has-beens, never-weres, and always-will-bes of classic rock as a writer/producer for the VH1 Radio Network. Since moving to New York from Seattle in 2001, she can be found singing bad karaoke songs in various New York bars and contributing to Gotham magazines such as *Shout*.

ANDREW G. ROSEN's writing career has been on hold after graduating with a degree in Media Studies and Journalism from Queens College. He has spent the past several years discovering the many facets of radio and has completed countless short stories, essays, and articles that he hopes to have published in the near future. Currently, he is the Production Manager for VH1 Satellite Radio where his love for music continues to be his guiding force.

ARTHUR D. SEGUNDEWITZ is a successful singer/songwriter from Bay City, Michigan, whose first album, *Pipe's Dream*, released on the Blind Raccoon label in 1985, won the Prairie Radio Award for Best Folk Album of the Year. A pioneer of indie consciousness, Segundewitz self-released many of his own recordings on cassette during the eighties and wrote for *Sound Choice* 'zine. He's more recently become actively involved with the dissemination of music through the MP3 format.

QUINTON SKINNER is also the author of *VH1 Behind the Music: Casualties of Rock*, the parenting memoir *Do I Look Like a Daddy to You?*, and the upcoming novel *Amnesia Nights*. He lives with his family in Minneapolis.

MATTHEW SPECKTOR began his descent into bankruptcy at age fifteen, coincident with his discovery of bootleg LPs. He has since overspent his allowance in New York, London, San Francisco, and elsewhere, forever in search of the unheard music. His wife is a very patient person.

HEATHER STAS loves music. Her passion for it started at a very young age while growing up on the New Jersey shore. At age thirteen, she saw her first concert, Bob Dylan, with opening band, the Alarm, which was "a moment that changed me forever." A few years later, she became active in her local independent music scene, which prompted her to initiate the plan for a career in music and radio. She started her life as a music journalist in New York after graduation, entering the doors of MTV in 1997. In 2000, she helped form its sister network, VH1 Radio, for which she is now a producer. Over those years, Heather has performed countless interviews with those in music and in film as well as still lending a hand to unsigned bands. Her love of interviewing people led Heather to one of her most recent assignments—working with Tori Amos on projects associated with her album *Scarlet's Walk*.

ERIC WYBENGA is the author of *Dead to the Core: An Almanack of the Grateful Dead* and a frequent writer on music. He lives in Brooklyn, New York.